Progress
Against Poverty

Progress
Against Poverty

*Sustaining Mexico's
Progresa-Oportunidades Program*

Santiago Levy

BROOKINGS INSTITUTION PRESS
Washington, D.C.

Library of Congress Cataloging-in-Publication data
Levy, Santiago.
    Progress against poverty : sustaining Mexico's Progresa-Oportunidades program /
Santiago Levy.
        p.   cm.
    Summary: "Case study of Progresa-Oportunidades that describes the origins, objectives,
and institutional design and scope of Progresa; provides a broad assessment of results to
date; discusses the main challenges faced by the program in the future; and makes some
suggestions for poverty programs drawn from the main lessons of the study"—Provided
by publisher.
    Includes bibliographical references and index.
    ISBN-13: 978-0-8157-5221-9 (pbk. : alk. paper)
    ISBN-10: 0-8157-5221-0 (pbk. : alk. paper)
    1. Poor—Mexico. 2. Poor—Government policy—Mexico. 3. Programa de Educación,
Salud y Alimentación (Mexico City, Mexico)—Evaluation. 4. Economic assistance,
Domestic—Mexico. 5. Poverty—Mexico. I. Title.
    HC140.P6P483 2006
    362.5'580972—dc22   2006028230

9 8 7 6 5 4 3 2 1

The paper used in this publication meets minimum requirements of the
American National Standard for Information Sciences—Permanence of Paper
for Printed Library Materials: ANSI Z39.48-1992.

Typeset in Sabon

Composition by Cynthia Stock
Silver Spring, Maryland

Printed by R. R. Donnelley
Harrisonburg, Virginia

Contents

v

Foreword

When I became president of the World Bank in 1995, I was determined to put the goal of global poverty reduction at the front and center of the mission of the institution, which I was to lead for ten years. With more than one billion people living in abject poverty on less than one dollar a day, I felt strongly that the international community had to focus its attention much more squarely on reducing the plight of the poor—and on the extraordinary contribution that they can make to create a better world. I was convinced that to achieve the goal of global poverty reduction, we had to adopt a comprehensive approach that incorporated the key dimensions of good governance, strong institutions, and local ownership. Such an approach would have to be multifaceted, covering the many sectors and areas of economic and social life; it would have to be designed to attack poverty with measurable results, on a scale commensurate with the problem; and it would have to be sustained over time. I also knew that we should not and could not start from scratch but should build on the experience of many decades of development effort by the countries in which we worked.

I was therefore very excited when I first encountered an innovative program in Mexico that was then known as Progresa. This program met many of the expectations that I had nurtured regarding successful poverty reduction initiatives: it was homegrown, based on solid economic and social analysis, comprehensive in approach, and sensitive to the institutional and political realities of the country. Most impressive of all, it was designed from the start to have a measurable and sustained impact, reaching over time virtually all of the poorest members of Mexican society. Progresa is built on a simple idea: rather than just transfer income to the poor through various subsidies for food, transportation, electricity, and the like, it is better to transfer income directly, in monetary terms. However, if transfers are to help break the intergenerational transmission of poverty, receipt must be contingent on investments by the poor themselves in their own nutrition, health, and education. In sum, Progresa transforms a pure welfare approach into an offer of aid today that is linked with investments for the future—a future that is built on the direct participation of poor households in overcoming their conditions.

Over the years, other international organizations as well as the World Bank have made use of this very impressive and successful Mexican initiative to assist other countries. Today, programs like Progresa are being carried out in more than twenty developing countries as part of their poverty reduction strategy, and many more are in the process of starting a program based on Progresa's principles and objectives. At the same time, Progresa's rigorous emphasis on evaluation has set a standard for poverty reduction programs in the developing world.

A key factor in the success of Progresa's start-up was the visionary leadership of Mexico's President Ernesto Zedillo, supported by an outstanding young Mexican economist, Santiago Levy, who was instrumental in designing Progresa's basic approach and who also was entrusted with the task of implementing the program. President Vicente Fox deserves much credit for having continued the program—under its new name, Oportunidades—in such an effective way that it has reached national scale. At this juncture in mid-2006, the program, which now has operated for almost ten years, faces perhaps its greatest challenge. This challenge is twofold: first, the program must be sustained by the new incoming presidential administration in Mexico; second, it must continue to focus sharply on its objectives, persisting in the essential tasks of eradicating undernutrition, ensuring that all poor children and youngsters successfully complete their education, and ensuring better health for all. Put differently, the challenge for Oportunidades, having now been scaled up to cover practically all poor Mexicans, is ensuring its own continuity and sustainability.

In this book, Santiago Levy presents arguments that can help Mexico meet those twin challenges in the coming months and years. He first provides background material, expounds the economic arguments for the new approach, and describes the scope and scale of Progresa, which now redistributes income and provides nutrition, health, and educational benefits to nearly one of every four Mexicans. He then pulls together the available and far-reaching evidence on the success of Progresa-Oportunidades, summarizing a large set of external qualitative and quantitative evaluations of the various impacts of the program.

The more novel aspects of the book, however, are those that center on the program's institutional design and its future perspective. Levy explains how the elements of transparency, accountability, and credibility have been incorporated in the program since its inception, to contribute not only to good program operation but also to program continuity and sustainability. He documents on one hand how the program was designed to keep it outside the realm of partisan politics and, on the other, why this kind of income transfer program needs to be made compatible with other social programs for the poor. Now that the first young people are "graduating" from the program better nourished, more educated, and in better health than they otherwise would have been, there is a risk that they will face underemployment or unemployment and with it, disappointed expectations and pressures to emigrate. The challenge is to construct a coherent poverty reduction strategy whereby economic opportunities and incentives are aligned to promote productivity and effort while avoiding situations in which the poor are inadvertently locked in low-productivity occupations as a result of participating in numerous well-intentioned but uncoordinated social programs. Given his long-standing involvement in the design, implementation, and evaluation of Progresa-Oportunidades, Santiago Levy is uniquely qualified to offer cogent insight and advice on how best to meet that challenge.

In addition to its substantive and timely input to what I hope will be a lively and productive debate in Mexico about the country's poverty reduction strategy, this volume can serve more broadly as a model of effective design of large-scale sustainable poverty reduction programs in developing countries. Over the years I have encountered numerous successful development programs of a scale too small or duration too short to make a notable and lasting impact on poverty. That is why, in addition to the technical aspects of a poverty program, institutional elements that can ensure adequate scale and continuity are equally indispensable for effective poverty alleviation.

Santiago Levy's book was commissioned by the Wolfensohn Center at the Brookings Institution. The center's mission is to carry out action-oriented research to find answers to the following question: How can successful development interventions—strategies, policies, programs, and projects—be designed and implemented so that their impact is scaled up and sustained to solve key development challenges at a national, regional, and global scale? With that goal in mind, the author set out not only to address the question of whether Progresa-Oportunidades has succeeded in reducing poverty in Mexico but also to answer another key question: what economic, institutional, and political factors in the design, implementation, and evaluation of the program have permitted it to make such an extraordinary impact and to achieve such scale and sustainability over the last ten years? The Wolfensohn Center plans to build on Santiago Levy's unique insights by developing an in-depth research program on large-scale antipoverty programs in the developing world. Such programs are essential instruments in the most important fight of all: the fight to end poverty worldwide.

James D. Wolfensohn
Washington, D.C.
September 2006

Acknowledgments

I would like to express my gratitude to James D. Wolfensohn, who as president of the World Bank gave me the opportunity to share the experience of Progresa-Oportunidades with the governments of Brazil and Egypt, and who later invited me to write the paper that became this book for the initiative launched under his name at the Brookings Institution. Johannes Linn, executive director of the Wolfensohn Center at Brookings, has been extremely supportive, and discussions with him and members of his team over the last few months have been useful and constructive. Evelyne Rodriguez read the manuscript and gave me helpful critical comments and suggestions, and Jose Angel González provided valuable research assistance. Eileen Hughes of the Brookings Institution Press was an excellent editor. My greatest debt, however, is with my colleagues in Mexico. I especially would like to mention three dear friends with whom I had the privilege to share, more than a decade ago, the initial work on what eventually would be Progresa: Jose Antonio Alvarado, the late Enrique Dávila, and Evelyne Rodriguez.

Progress
Against Poverty

Introduction

In 1997 Mexico launched a new incentive-based poverty reduction program, initially known as Progresa and now as Oportunidades, to enhance the human capital of those living in extreme poverty. The program started under the administration of President Ernesto Zedillo, with initial coverage of 300,000 families in 6,344 localities in twelve states and a budget of US$58.8 million (see tables 2-1 and 2-5 in chapter 2).[1]

At that time, Progresa-Oportunidades was a novel initiative, inasmuch as it

—sought to substitute cash income transfers for income transfers in the form of targeted or generalized food subsidies (through price discounts, price controls, in-kind distributions of food items, and the like), giving beneficiary families complete freedom in their spending decisions

—conditioned the receipt of cash transfers on specific patterns of behavior by beneficiary households

—packaged nutritional, health, and educational benefits together to exploit their complementarities

1. From its beginning in July 1997 to mid-2002, the program was known as Progresa; since then it has been known as Oportunidades. Some papers and publications refer to it by one designation and some by the other. In this text the program is referred to primarily as Progresa-Oportunidades.

—adopted a life-cycle approach to avoid long-term welfare dependence

—included evaluations of program operations and impacts as part of program design

—applied strict guidelines for selecting beneficiaries

—delivered benefits directly to beneficiaries, with no intermediaries.

At the end of 2005, under the administration of President Vicente Fox, Progresa-Oportunidades covered 5 million families, representing almost 24 percent of the country's population and practically all households living in extreme poverty. It operated in more than 86,000 localities in all thirty-one states of the country, with a budget of US$2.8 billion (see tables 2-1 and 2-5). Over the course of this period, many scholars evaluated the program, principally in terms of its impact on beneficiaries' consumption, health, nutrition, education, investment, intrahousehold relationships, use of labor time, and migration patterns. They also evaluated the program's methods of targeting eligible households and its effects on poverty indicators. Results to date have been positive; perhaps one could say very positive. Because of its novel approach and its results so far, Progresa-Oportunidades has at times been mentioned as an initiative that may provide useful lessons for reducing poverty in other countries.

Purpose of the Study

This book presents a case study of Progresa-Oportunidades, written under the assumption that, at least so far, the program can be considered a successful development initiative. Its purpose is to contribute to knowledge of how successful development initiatives can be designed and implemented so that they are sustained, adapted, scaled-up, and replicated to solve key development challenges. With that aim in mind, the book centers its attention on the

—main factors that have contributed to program continuity and sustainability over almost a decade, including the incentives of the domestic political system and multilateral institutions

—policies that have allowed the program to operate at the national level and attain its large scale

—public information mechanisms that have supported program implementation

—the role of evaluation in program scale-up and continuity and the lessons of the randomized approach used in the evaluation process

—future challenges that the program faces

—potential lessons that the program might provide, including insights on the transferability of programs of this nature to other countries.

Other aspects of the program—particularly the more technical issues of poverty measurement, algorithms for identifying beneficiaries, and techniques for impact evaluations—are either ignored or touched on only as necessary for the purposes of the study.[2]

Chapters 1 and 2 describe the origins, objectives, and scope of Progresa-Oportunidades, drawing from Levy and Rodriguez (2004). Chapter 3 provides a broad assessment of the main program results to date, bringing together the results of quantitative and qualitative evaluations of rural and urban areas carried out from 1998 to mid-2006, including results of reports available only in Spanish. Chapter 4 describes institutional design features of the program. Chapter 5 discusses the primary future challenges that the program faces. Finally, chapter 6 makes some suggestions for poverty programs drawn from the main lessons learned through Progresa-Oportunidades.

2. Levy and Rodriguez (2004) provides a poverty profile of Mexico, a description of the country's poverty alleviation strategy and programs, and an analysis of the motivation, design, and results of Progresa-Oportunidades up to 2003. Since then the program has expanded its scope and coverage, and more evaluation studies have been (and are being) conducted.

CHAPTER ONE

Program
Background

Mexico, like many other developing countries, has made a determined effort over many decades to combat poverty and reduce income inequality. From the human capital perspective, that effort has been evident principally in programs to improve the food consumption, health status, and education of the poor.[1]

Despite those programs, in the mid-1990s an estimated 24 percent of all households, representing almost 30 percent of the country's population (poor households are, on average, larger than others), lived in extreme poverty. Conditions in rural areas, where more than 50 percent of all households lived in poverty, were worse than in urban areas, where the poverty rate was 14 percent.[2] Furthermore, when indicators of the depth and severity of poverty were considered, it was clear that the rural poor were not only more numerous but also relatively worse off than the urban poor. Similar results obtained when non-income indicators of welfare were used: nutritional status, infant mortality, illiteracy rates, access to and use of health and educational services, and the like.

Limitations of Food Subsidies

To increase poor households' food consumption, in the mid-1990s Mexico's federal government ran fifteen food subsidy programs: four were

---

1. See Levy (1994) for a description of poverty programs in Mexico up to the mid-1990s.
2. Levy and Rodriguez (2004).

generalized, and eleven targeted different urban and rural populations. These programs, which were operated by ten distinct ministries or agencies, were of varying coverage and scope. (See table 1-1 for program budget allocations for 1996, the year before Progresa began.)[3]

Seven observations can be made about these programs at that time. First, given the distribution of poor households, there was an imbalance in the distribution of budget funds between urban and rural areas: more than 75 percent of the total budget was channeled to urban areas, where less than 40 percent of the poor lived. Second, there was an imbalance in the amounts of targeted and generalized subsidies, with almost two-thirds of all resources channeled to the latter. In fact, over half of the total budget was absorbed by the generalized bread and tortilla subsidies in urban areas, where most of the income transfer was captured by non-poor households.[4]

Third, extensive population dispersion made it difficult to deliver food subsides—generalized or targeted—in rural areas. In 1995 approximately 2.7 million people lived in 150,000 localities of less than 100 inhabitants; an additional 7.8 million resided in 33,000 localities of between 100 and 500 people.[5] A majority of these localities are marginalized, and a large share of the rural poor live there; many also are in mountainous terrain and difficult to reach, given the lack of rural roads.[6] Under such circumstances, delivering in-kind food subsidies was inefficient (high transportation costs, low volume per locality, few storage facilities, and so on) and enforcing price controls or price subsidies was administratively infeasible. Therefore, channeling food subsidies to the rural poor was more costly and complex than channeling them to the urban poor, even without taking into account the political pressure that the relatively more concentrated and organized urban poor could exert. Few benefits reached poor rural residents.

---

3. Unless otherwise stated, all figures in this book are in 2005 pesos; when figures are in U.S. dollars, the average exchange rate for 2005 was 10.7 pesos to one dollar.

4. That was because both bread and tortilla are consumed widely by all segments of the population. The Lorenz curve for tortilla consumption is almost a 45 degree line. Tortillas, made from maize, are a staple for all consumers and therefore are a very inefficient instrument for transferring income to the poor. Levy and Rodriguez (2004) estimated that of every peso allocated to the generalized urban tortilla subsidy, less than 15 centavos reached the urban poor. The situation with bread, made from wheat, was worse, because the better-off consumed more bread than the poor and almost no bread was consumed in rural areas.

5. Dávila and Levy (2004, table 1).

6. See Dávila and Levy (2004) for more details.

Table 1-1. *Budget for Food Subsidy Programs, 1996*
Millions of 2005 pesos

Type of subsidies[a]	Urban areas	Rural areas	Total
Generalized	13,614	3,169	16,783
Targeted	6,843	2,903	9,746
Total	20,457	6,072	26,529

Source: Author's calculations based on data in Levy and Rodriguez (2004).

a. Generalized subsidies include those for bread and tortillas in urban areas and for maize and maize flour in rural areas, as well as price discounts for selected food items (cooking oil, beans, and so on) in public stores located mostly in rural areas. Targeted subsidies include those for milk, tortillas (in addition to the generalized subsidy), and school breakfasts, mostly in urban areas, and for community kitchens, food baskets for indigenous communities, and other minor programs in rural areas.

Fourth, a significant share of the total budget was absorbed by the administrative expenses of ministries and agencies in charge of the programs. Fifth, there was little coordination between agencies, leading to duplication of efforts and, in the case of targeted programs, difficulties in systematically identifying poor households because of the different methodologies used. One significant consequence of the concentration of resources and programs in urban areas, large inclusion and exclusion errors, and logistical problems in reaching remote rural areas was that in 1995 close to 60 percent of all poor rural families received no food support at all from the government.[7]

Sixth, with the exception of a few small targeted subsidies, food subsidy programs and nutritional or health interventions were run independently of each other, and they did not focus adequately on the most vulnerable members of the family (generally, children under two years of age and pregnant or nursing women).[8] Those shortcomings reduced their

7. The urban bias in food programs was large. Aside from the budget numbers mentioned, Levy and Rodriguez (2004, p. 25) documents that the milk distribution program reached only 7 percent of all poor rural households; the food package program, 24.2 percent; and the school breakfast program, only 8.5 percent. The authors also show that even the public rural stores where food items were sold at price discounts had a short reach: they were present in only 30 percent of all highly marginalized rural communities. In urban areas, inclusion and exclusion errors were large. The authors report that the Ministry of the Comptrollership found that the targeted tortilla program had an inclusion error of 20 percent (50 percent in Mexico City) and that the milk program had an inclusion error of 50 percent.

8. In principle, the school breakfast program targeted children. However, the program could reach only children who actually attended school, and it provided benefits only for children aged five years or more; by design, it could not reach all poor children in the critical first two or three years of life. Furthermore, the program reached only 25 percent of all

impact on the poor, since in many cases increasing the amount of food available would not necessarily translate into better nutrition and health status for all members of the household.[9] Seventh, program operations and impact were not subject to systematic evaluation; on the whole, ministries and agencies operated with great discretionary authority and little accountability.

More generally, food subsidy programs, despite being considered nutritional programs by some observers, were at that time essentially a mechanism to transfer income to the poor.[10] Nevertheless, since Mexico's very unequal distribution of income translates into a very unequal distribution of consumption, food subsidies (and, more generally, consumption subsidies) are a very ineffective and inefficient mechanism for transferring income.[11] They are ineffective for at least two reasons:

—Even if the subsidy is complete (that is, the food item is free), the quantity consumed is finite, limiting the size of the subsidy (that is, income transfer) received by the poor.

—If the subsidy is not complete (that is, if the food item has a positive price), the size of the subsidy received by poor households is limited by their income and by the need to spend on other goods and services.

---

marginalized communities in Mexico. National nutritional surveys indicate that between 1974 and 1996 the prevalence of malnutrition among children under five fell slightly, from 50.7 percent to 47.8 percent, while mild malnutrition declined from 33.3 percent to 28.6 percent. However, moderate to severe malnutrition rose from 17.4 to 19.3 percent. Data were taken from Levy and Rodriguez (2004, p. 27).

9. Three considerations are in order here. First, it is important to differentiate between malnutrition and under-nutrition. The former is an imbalance in the diet reflecting the absence of some key nutrients; the latter reflects generally low overall food intake. In Mexico there is a relative abundance of vegetable proteins in the diet of the poor (coming from maize and beans, among other sources); there is a lack of some vitamins, iron, iodine, zinc, and folic acid. The second consideration has to do with the unhealthy conditions in which the poor at times live (including the absence of potable water, sewage facilities, and the like), which implies that, paraphrasing Streeten, giving the poor access to more food may satisfy only the needs of the parasites lodged in their stomachs (Streeten, 1989). The third has to do with intrahousehold inequality, implying that additional food for the household would not necessarily translate into additional food for all members of the household. None of the food programs at that time addressed these issues.

10. Besley and Kanbur (1988) studies the relationship between food subsidies and income transfers. If the quantity of the subsidized food item consumed is inframarginal (that is, less than would be consumed in the absence of the subsidy), the equivalence between a pure lump-sum income transfer and the food subsidy is complete. If the subsidy is given through price discounts, there is also a substitution effect, proportional to the size of the price elasticity of the good subsidized.

11. Dávila and Levy (2003).

The inefficiency of food subsidies as an income transfer mechanism, on the other hand, stems from the fact that a small share of spending on the subsidized food item by a high-income household may exceed, in absolute terms, a large share of spending on the same food item by a poor household, implying that a large share of the subsidy is captured by middle- and high-income groups.[12]

Of course, to the extent that there was no other mechanism to transfer income to the poor, existing food programs at that time played an important role in helping the poor households that did receive them. Clearly, not trying to correct inequalities in income distribution (and hence food consumption) was not an option. The challenge therefore was not to eliminate the programs, but to replace them with another instrument that would be more effective and efficient in transferring income to the poor and have greater positive impacts on their health and nutritional status.

Uneven Achievements in Health and Education

Despite the government's efforts to improve the health status of Mexico's population, results in the mid-1990s were uneven. There had been some very important achievements: for example, over the previous three decades, life expectancy at birth increased from fifty-two to seventy-two years, and vaccination programs reached more than 95 percent of the population, reducing considerably the incidence of preventable diseases like poliomyelitis, tetanus, whooping cough, and tuberculosis.[13] Other nationwide indicators showed similar advances.

Nevertheless, notable differences remained in health and nutrition indicators across income levels. For example, the infant mortality rate for the rural poor was 165 percent higher than for the urban non-poor; in the

---

12. That is exactly what happened with the bread and tortilla subsidy. Hence, in order to concentrate a food subsidy on the poor population, broad food categories should not be subsidized. Instead, specific food items consumed only by poor households (such as coarse maize flour instead of fine maize flour) must be identified. Doing so requires distinguishing between "luxury" and "popular" categories of food items, which normally imposes very high administrative costs and may induce cheating (for example, making one good appear to be the other in order to get the subsidy) and even corruption. But even if making such a distinction is feasible, such carefully defined food items usually will absorb a small share of the total spending budget of the household, highlighting the ineffectiveness of the food subsidy as an instrument for transferring income.

13. Levy and Rodriguez (2004).

500 most marginalized municipalities, the average height of children was almost 5 percent below the national mean, a result probably due to the cumulative effects of nutritional deficiencies.[14]

Access to reproductive health services also was uneven, with significant implications for poverty. Levy and Rodriguez (2004) documents that only 56 percent of poor women used some method of birth control at that time, in contrast to 71 percent of non-poor women, and the fertility rate for poor women was 5.1 children, more than double the rate of 2.5 children for non-poor women. In fact, the fertility rate for poor women in 1995 was equivalent to the national rate in 1979, implying a lag of more than fifteen years in the reduction of birth rates and family size among poor households (that is, a lagged demographic transition). As a result, in the mid-1990s poor women had their first child at the age of 19.7 years, on average, while the average for non-poor women was 22.5 years. At that age the difference translates into a significantly larger family size.[15]

More generally, by the mid-1990s the poor still had inadequate access to preventive health services, insufficient information about basic health care, and low use of health services. These three factors, together with deficient hygiene and scarce resources for food consumption, exacerbated morbidity and malnutrition. Better health care provision by itself, however, does not help prevent simple pathologies if families continue to have inadequate access to food or unbalanced diets. Many simple health problems can be treated more easily by providing better nutrition and earlier diagnostics, but doing so requires stimulating the demand for services as well as improving their supply. Stimulating demand was not an objective of the health strategies followed at that time.

Achievements in education also were both notable and uneven. By 1996, 92 percent of all children between the ages of six and fourteen received a basic education. More than 80 percent of children who began primary school completed it successfully, with a drop-out rate of 3 percent; moreover, 87 percent of those completing primary school enrolled in secondary school.[16]

14. In the first few years of life, nutritional deficiencies may cause permanent anthropometric and cognitive underdevelopment, generating long-lasting deficits in school or work performance (Levy and Rodriguez 2004).

15. In 1994, average poor household size was 5.8 members and non-poor size was 4.3 members; in turn, the dependency index (ratio of household members who do not work to those who do) was 3.3 for the poor and 2.1 for the non-poor. See Levy and Rodriguez (2004).

16. Levy and Rodriguez (2004). In Mexico, basic education includes six years of primary school and three years of secondary school.

In poor households there were significant lags, however. In 1996 one in every ten children between the ages of eight and twelve did not attend school; in the thirteen-to-seventeen range the ratio was close to one in two. Girls were markedly less schooled than boys: attendance of fourteen-year-old girls was 10 percent lower than for boys of the same age, and average years of schooling for girls aged fifteen to seventeen was 4.7 years, in contrast to 5.5 for boys of the same age.[17]

The schooling indicators, like the health indicators, had substantive implications for poverty. In the mid-1990s the income level in Mexico for households in which the family head had a basic school education was twice that for households whose family head did not; therefore deficiencies in school attendance among the poor had implications for life-time earnings. Deficiencies in education also had negative effects on health. Evidence showed, for instance, that family care and eating habits suffered when mothers were less educated. Although some programs at that time promoted school attendance by poor children, their coverage was very small.[18]

Analytical Advances in Poverty Policy

The 1980s and 1990s saw the emergence of a large body of work by economists, sociologists, nutritionists, and other researchers that led to progressively better understanding of some of the determinants of poverty.[19] In matters related to human capital, this literature emphasized the links between food intake, nutrition, health, and education. A parallel literature contributed to clarifying the role of food subsidies as a mechanism to transfer income to the poor.

In particular, interactions, spillover effects, or externalities between food consumption, nutrition, health, and education showed the presence of large complementarities among these goods. That in turn suggested that an integrated rather than isolated approach to delivering services

17. Levy and Rodriguez (2004).

18. A notable effort in this regard was Children in Solidarity, a component of the much larger National Solidarity Program begun by President Carlos Salinas in 1988. This program granted scholarships to poor children who attended school, and its experience was very important for Progresa-Oportunidades later on. Still, in 1996 less than 5 percent of all poor children received a scholarship under the program; see Levy and Rodriguez (2004).

19. See Lipton and Ravallion (1995) for an excellent summary of results at that time and Levy (1994) for the empirical evidence available for Mexico.

could be more effective and efficient in tackling the nutritional, health, and educational needs of the poor. These interactions are briefly discussed here, as they provide the analytical backbone for the integrated approach taken by Progresa-Oportunidades.

First, there is an interaction among food supply, nutrition, and health. Since many poor families live in unhealthy conditions and experience a high incidence of diarrhea and other intestinal diseases, access to more food need not translate into better nutritional status. To achieve that, better health conditions, including environmental health, are essential. To improve nutrition, therefore, it may be insufficient to transfer income to poor families, as did most food subsidy programs in Mexico at that time.

Second, there is an interaction among infant mortality, fertility, and health. Low use of reproductive health services and high infant mortality, which are associated with higher fertility, have delayed the demographic transition in poor households. That delay in turn contributes to the persistence of poverty due to greater dispersion of resources within the family, reduced health of mothers, and diminished individual attention by parents to their children's educational, emotional, and social development.

A third interaction occurs among family size, education, and health. The costs of sending children to school can be too high for poor families (even if there is no tuition) because of the costs of school supplies and transportation and of the forgone contributions of children to household tasks or monetary income. Poor children, therefore, may not fully benefit from programs that improve the quantity and quality of educational services. As noted above, that has medium-term implications, since poor children eventually enter the labor market at a disadvantage. At the same time, more education for women delays the age at which they give birth to their first child; contributes to reducing infant mortality; reduces the frequency of pregnancies; and exerts a positive effect on the nutrition and health of children.

Fourth and last, there is an interaction between low income and risk aversion. Living under the constant threat of a sudden drop in income—and hence consumption—probably makes poor families, on average, more risk averse than non-poor families. That affects their ability to participate in the labor market by searching for better jobs, or it may limit the possibility of migrating to other communities or of introducing new crops or improved technologies. Poor families may be induced to cling to small parcels of land or traditional farming methods that generate lower but safer returns, limiting the benefits that they may be able to obtain from rural development programs or urban job training programs. For those reasons, reducing poor households' uncertainty regarding food consumption could allow them to engage in riskier productive projects or investments with longer planning horizons (including children's education).[20]

These analytical developments imply that programs that provide for the needs of the poor in an isolated or partial fashion may not attain the central objective of developing poor families' capabilities, even if they reach their beneficiaries adequately (which did not occur in many cases in Mexico at that time). Research results suggested that large welfare gains could be obtained instead by combining food subsidies and isolated health and educational interventions in an integrated approach that tapped their complementarities.

Research also suggested that to break the vicious cycle of poverty it was essential not only to subsidize food (that is, to transfer purchasing power) but simultaneously to give poor households more certainty about the availability of income to buy food or other necessities; to deliver more information on hygiene and reproductive health; to provide alternative sources of income for present consumption in order to replace income earned by children, allowing them to go to school more regularly, better fed, and for longer periods of time; to modify households' structure of health risks by inducing families to have more frequent and systematic contact with health service providers; to reduce their perception of vulnerability so that they can bear more risk and perhaps save and invest in new projects; to make them feel secure with a family of reduced size; and to allow them to devote more time and resources to each child. And because delivering the benefits simultaneously rather than separately would tap their substantive complementarities, in principle larger welfare gains would be observed by following an integrated approach.

Yet another body of research, and Mexico's own experience, pointed toward the need to involve poor families directly in overcoming their difficult circumstances.[21] To do so it was necessary to expand their freedom

20. The 2006 World Development Report, "Equity and Development," provides a good summary of research results indicating that in the presence of imperfections in land, labor, capital, and insurance markets, inequality and poverty translate into reduced investment by the poor (and, in some cases, overinvestment by the non-poor in relatively less profitable projects); see World Bank (2005, pp. 89–104).

21. See a volume sponsored by the World Bank: *Voices of the Poor: Can Anyone Hear Us?* Narayan and others (2000).

by giving them greater control over their own resources, better information, increased opportunities to participate, more choice in spending their income transfers, and, simultaneously, more responsibility.

It was also important, finally, to avoid generating lasting dependence on income transfers. Experience from other countries had shown that making pure income transfers just because the recipients were poor could reduce their incentives to work and invest, inadvertently leading a subset of potentially able and productive citizens to permanent dependence on public welfare. To avoid that outcome, income transfers should be designed to be transitory investments in the human capital of the poor. They should take a life-cycle approach, helping poor households in the more critical aspects of each stage of their lives but always with the view that they should have incentives to earn a sufficient level of income through their own efforts to eventually pull themselves out of poverty.

A challenge at that time, however, was to bring academic researchers' analytical insights and individual nation's best practices together in a unified conceptual framework in order to incorporate that knowledge systematically in the design of a poverty program. For reasons that are explored below, Mexico did so in the mid-1990s, while including some institutional innovations that sought to give the program the scale and continuity necessary to have a lasting impact on the poor.

Motivation for Change and Implications of a New Approach

In 1994–95, during the transition from the administration of President Carlos Salinas to that of President Ernesto Zedillo, Mexico's economy suffered a substantial setback. After experiencing great political uncertainty (a guerrilla uprising in Chiapas and the murder of the PRI presidential candidate, among other events), in December 1994 Mexico suffered a major macroeconomic crisis. The crisis developed rapidly, and it resulted in a drop in GDP of approximately 6 percent over the course of 1995, the largest reduction in economic activity in more than five decades.

There was wide agreement among policymakers at that time that a crisis of such magnitude would have very negative implications for the poor in Mexico. There was less agreement among them, however, about how to respond to the crisis. To some members of the Cabinet, strengthening the existing programs was the best course of action. Others, particularly officials from the Finance Ministry, argued on the basis of the research results presented above that existing programs, particularly the set of generalized and targeted food subsidies that were in place at that time, were inadequate to protect the poor during the crisis.[22]

While the economic crisis created the immediate motivation for change—and the beginning of a new administration naturally created a political climate that facilitated change—the accumulation of empirical evidence, administrative experience, and analytical arguments was fundamental in gradually persuading the members of the Cabinet to make substantive adjustments to the existing food subsidy and related poverty programs.[23] The challenge was to design a rapid short-term response to the crisis with the existing instruments while setting the basis for a medium-term strategy that, aside from protecting the poor from the transitory shock, could foster a sustained increase in their standard of living.

The absence of effective mechanisms to protect the poor created a dilemma for the government: on one hand, although increasing the scope and coverage of existing programs in the very short run would show that measures were being taken to protect the poor, it would make it more difficult to phase them out later on and would reduce the credibility of the government's commitment to revamp food subsidy policy; not doing so, on the other hand, would give the impression that the government was insensitive to the needs of the poor. And while this was mostly a political dilemma, because in fact there was little that the government could do in the very short run to effectively alleviate the impact of the crisis on the poor, the policy response was important to the poverty alleviation strategy, given the constraints that it could impose on future courses of action that could bring much larger welfare gains to the poor.

---

22. To recapitulate: most resources were channeled through generalized subsidies, with a large share of the benefits captured by the non-poor; targeted programs had very limited coverage in rural areas and large inclusion and exclusion errors in urban areas; it was not feasible in the short run (nor desirable in the medium run) to extend the network of public rural stores where food items were sold at a discount; and no agency or ministry had the ability to rapidly identify and deliver income transfers to the set of poor households, particularly in rural areas, that were not covered by these programs.

23. Subjective considerations, although by nature difficult to measure, also played a part. At least among some policymakers there was a sense that these programs had generated corruption; that there were large deviations of benefits for unintended purposes (for example, subsidized maize flour intended for tortilla consumption would be exported or used for animal feed instead); and that the roster of beneficiaries of targeted programs in urban areas had been manipulated for political gain. According to data from the Central Bank (which in Mexico is in charge of the official price statistics), the price ceiling on tortillas associated with the generalized subsidy was observed in only fourteen of thirty-two states (Levy and Rodriguez 2004).

Therefore, along with managing the short-term macroeconomic ramifications of the crisis, which included a rather modest expansion of some existing programs, the incoming administration embarked on the design of a new approach to food subsidies in particular and related poverty programs more generally that would be able to

—incorporate the academic research results summarized earlier

—take advantage of the lessons and experiences of Mexico's own programs

—use the crisis as a motivation for change.[24]

While it was commonly acknowledged that poverty alleviation required more budgetary resources, the difficult budgetary situation at that time contributed to strengthening the view of Finance Ministry officials and others who argued that the quality and effectiveness of public spending in general and of poverty programs in particular should be a matter of greater concern. And the fact that the president himself had been the minister of budgeting and planning in the previous administration—and an economist by training—helped immensely in dealing with these considerations.

Building consensus inside the Cabinet was a gradual process, and the consensus achieved was never complete. As elaborated on in chapter 4, a fairly radical departure from the status quo was being proposed, and presidential leadership was essential to the implementation and success of the program. In the course of various Cabinet discussions over 1995 and 1996, it became clear that in addition to a shift in thinking about the relationship among food subsidy programs, income transfers, and the human capital of the poor, a new approach would require reallocation of the budget for poverty programs; reorganization of the administrative apparatus devoted to poverty alleviation; new emphasis on evaluation and measurement of program results; and development of a new political relationship between the federal government and beneficiary households. Seven issues are worth discussing in this context.

First, it was clear that the limited scope of the subset of targeted programs that reached the poor was a major shortcoming. A national effort,

24. The government's tool kit also included programs not directly associated with human capital formation. There were transfer programs to poor rural households that owned some land (the PROCAMPO program), some urban and rural temporary employment programs, and some microcredit programs. These programs were also used as part of the immediate policy response, although none were really designed for that purpose. Chapter 3 describes some research that evaluates the role that Progresa-Oportunidades could play as a mechanism to protect the poor from transitory shocks.

which was the aim from the beginning, would succeed only if it reached all of the poor in a systematic and lasting way. A continuous and large-scale program imposed two requirements from the very beginning: quantification of the budgetary and administrative effort that the new approach implied, and identification of the conditions that could give continuity to the effort over the medium run.

Second, it was essential to clearly identify the target population, both in terms of the aggregate number of households to be reached and their geographical location. That implied establishing a single definition of persons living in extreme poverty and a single methodology to identify them, so that all federal agencies and ministries could focus on the same set of people. And that in turn implied a substantial reduction in the discretionary powers of ministries and agencies in the poverty-oriented programs under their jurisdiction, particularly with regard to selection of locations and beneficiaries.

Third, more budgetary efficiency was required, for four reasons:

—the tight budget conditions under which the government was operating at that time and would be operating under into the foreseeable medium term[25]

—the need for fiscal resources for other poverty programs (such as those investing in physical infrastructure, promoting productive opportunities, and so on)

—the potential for creating perverse incentives against work and effort by making multiple transfers through various programs

—the need to help ensure that the new combined income transfer/nutrition/health/education program would eventually become substantially larger than any single program in the past.

These four reasons implied, critically, that the new program would replace, not supplement, existing programs and that it would be financed to a large extent by the reallocation of existing resources. Put differently, the new program would be implemented "instead off" and not "in addition to" previous programs.

Fourth, creating the new program implied a significant reallocation of tasks and responsibilities among federal ministries and agencies. Such a shift would require large political resources, given that at times ministries

25. Aside from the constraints on the federal budget resulting from the short-run macroeconomic adjustment program to the 1994–95 crisis, the government also had to face the costs of reforming pensions and supporting financial institutions.

and agencies are driven by bureaucratic inertia or the desire for political gain, with little incentive to cooperate. An integrated program would require a coordinated collective response, which in turn would require giving an administrative unit control over operations on one hand, and giving stronger budgetary control to the Finance Ministry on the other. Both actions would require strong political backing. In Mexico's political structure that meant, foremost, direct involvement by the president in the discussions leading to the new approach and in implementation of and follow-up on the decisions taken. Without that leadership and support, it would have been impossible to phase out generalized food subsidies—particularly for tortillas, which had been in place for more than thirty years—and to close down agencies that had formed part of the federal government for a long time.

Fifth, a program that delivers income transfers in cash is different from one in which food items (bread, tortillas, milk, maize flour, beans) are purchased by poor households that may not know that the price they pay is below the market price because a subsidy is involved. And a program that requires certain behavior from the poor before they receive an income transfer is different from one in which they are given a transfer just because they are poor or they consume a given good. Progresa-Oportunidades was built, along with other considerations, on the recognition that poor households had to play a more substantive role in overcoming their circumstances; to that end, households were being given both increased freedom with regard to how they spent their income transfers and greater responsibility for taking the actions required to obtain the transfers.

Empowering beneficiaries in this fashion, however, had political implications. It involved a different relationship between the poor and the federal government. It required clear rules of operation and more transparency and accountability. And in a context of rapid democratization, it also required concrete assurances to Congress that the new effort would not be manipulated by the executive branch to obtain short-run political advantage; only then could congressional funding approval be expected. That is why developing clear and strict rules of operation, enforcing transparent and verifiable targeting mechanisms, requiring strict compliance with the conditions of the program, and incorporating credible impact and operational evaluations were, from the beginning, essential elements of the new program.

A sixth implication of the new approach, furthermore, was that poverty programs, or at least this new program, would no longer be the subject of agreements (*pactos*) between the government and to a large extent corporativist organizations that most commonly had been the government's interlocutors in various macroeconomic negotiations over the previous decade. That was a fundamental change, as the poor were not directly represented by any group in these *pactos*.[26] Henceforth, discussion of the nature, coverage, and resources for poverty programs, and for this new program in particular, would shift from ad hoc forums of that sort to Congress.

A seventh, final, consideration was associated with the need to overcome the "stop-go" problem that had plagued many good poverty alleviation efforts in the past, whereby programs launched under previous administrations were interrupted at the start of new ones, without having had the time to achieve their expected benefits. This consideration was particularly important in the context of a program designed to enhance the human capital of the poor, an effort that could come to full fruition only over the medium run.[27] Transparency, accountability, evaluation, and strict compliance with the operational rules of the program were to contribute to this purpose. But those elements had to be complemented by another program element of a qualitative and unavoidably more subjective nature: politically neutral operations that could permit a new administration (perhaps from a different political party) to continue with the program when it came into power. That required breaking with the perception, at least among some observers, that the new program would be used to enhance the status of the president or benefit his political party.[28]

The new approach, differently put, required a different kind of leadership

---

26. To correct the large macroeconomic imbalances triggered by the debt crisis of the 1980s, the Mexican government had relied on various "economic pacts" with representatives of workers, firms, peasants, and other actors. These *pactos*, as they were known in Mexico, served an extremely useful role as a coordinating mechanism to reduce inflationary expectations and to establish credible commitments among parties. At the time Progresa was being designed, economic policy was supported by one such *pacto*, signed in January 1995 and renewed in March 1995. Targets for food subsidies and similar programs were some of the elements negotiated in these *pactos*.

27. Clearly, achieving good health is a cumulative process, and temporary investments in nutrition are of little help. The same is true of education: children must be supported year after year until they complete high school if they are to benefit later from technical education or job training programs and to acquire a better paying job.

28. This perception was held, for instance, with regard to the National Solidarity Program (Pronasol, under its Spanish acronym) initiated by President Salinas (1989–94), the immediate predecessor to President Zedillo (1995–2000). Dresser (1994, pp. 262–63) argued that "Pronasol constitutes a central element in the governance formula of the Salinas administration" and that one of its aims was to "restructure the state and local level PRI [Partido Revolucionario Institucional] elites under more central control [author's translation]."

by the executive branch; a method for effectively coordinating activities of the implementing agencies and ministries within the executive branch; new relationships between beneficiary households and implementing agencies; less room for changing poverty programs as part of broader economic or political negotiations; and more active involvement by other actors, notably Congress and the academic research community.

These issues are discussed further in chapter 4 , but it is useful to point out here that they are inherent components of Progresa-Oportunidades, aside from the more analytical aspects of poverty policy mentioned above (that is, the elements justifying an integrated life-cycle approach). But to put the discussion in perspective, it is useful to turn first to a brief description of the objectives, components, and scope of the program (discussed in further detail in chapter 2) and to a summary of the program's results (chapter 3). Two final remarks, however, are in order.

First, Progresa-Oportunidades is not Mexico's poverty alleviation strategy. The program was part of a broad redesign of poverty policy, and it was launched with other measures to form an integrated strategy to combat poverty. Briefly, this strategy consists of a three-pronged approach that includes programs to enhance the human capital of the poor; to increase their income-earning opportunities through temporary employment, credit and rural development programs, and the like; and to improve the physical infrastructure in poor regions through housing, road-building, electrification, and water management projects, among others.[29] Progresa-Oportunidades focuses on the first component of the strategy, particularly on subsidizing the demand for health and educational services. The medium-term success of the program, however, also depends on the success of other components of the poverty strategy and on Mexico's overall growth and development.

Second, Progresa-Oportunidades will not directly increase growth, and it will not by itself eradicate poverty. The program can contribute to growth as it gradually fosters a healthier and more educated labor force and as it allows poor households to make more productive investments that have longer horizons and higher expected returns.[30] But that will not

---

29. Furthermore, one component of the strategy has programs besides Progresa-Oportunidades that center on improving the supply of health and educational services in poorer regions. See Levy and Rodriguez (2004) and Secretaría de Hacienda y Crédito Público (2000) for a description of these programs and the overall poverty strategy.

30. More broadly, policies that reduce inequality, as Progresa-Oportunidades does, also improve a country's institutions and policy environment in a way that is more conducive to long-term growth. See World Bank (2005).

have a first-order effect on the country's growth rate.[31] To eradicate poverty, Progresa-Oportunidades must be reinforced by the success of the other components of the poverty strategy and, equally, by macro- and microeconomic policies (regarding price and fiscal stability; incentives for investment, innovation, and job creation; and so on) that have a more direct bearing on growth than the program itself does. Although it may be an essential component of the solution, a single program cannot solve a problem that has multiple causes.

31. The first two deciles of the income distribution receive less than 2.5 percent of aggregate income in Mexico (Levy 1997). If all poor households' income (net of Progresa-Oportunidades transfers) increased by 5 percent a year, aggregate income would increase by, at most, an additional 0.12 percent a year over the growth rate without the program (clearly an overly optimistic assessment). The 5 percent figure comes from one of the evaluation studies, which show that Progresa-Oportunidades–induced investments may generate rates of return of this order of magnitude; see Gertler, Martinez, and Rubio (2005) and chapter 3 of this volume. The program also can affect growth through the higher potential productivity of labor, and that effect could be more substantial. However, such an effect would occur only if the more educated program workers find more productive jobs, which is something that Progresa-Oportunidades facilitates but does not guarantee.

CHAPTER TWO

Program Objectives and Scope

Progresa-Oportunidades seeks to break the vicious cycle of poverty in all extremely poor households, rural and urban, in Mexico. In particular, the program's objectives are to

—improve the health and nutritional status of poor households, particularly of their more vulnerable members: children under the age of five and pregnant and nursing women

—contribute to children's and young people's completion of their primary, secondary, and high school education

—integrate education, health, and nutrition interventions, so that children's school performance is not affected by ill health or malnourishment or by the need to work, either inside or outside the home

—redistribute income to families in extreme poverty, increasing their certainty of having a minimum level of consumption

—encourage the responsibility and active participation of parents and all members of the family in improving their own and their children's education, health, and nutritional status by giving them sufficient information on these issues and complete freedom with regard to their decisions about family size, children's education, and spending patterns.

Progresa-Oportunidades is a targeted program. Poor households are identified through a point system based on household demographics, assets, and other measurable characteristics that, in principle, cannot be manipulated by beneficiaries.[1] The targeting mechanism, although not problem free, tries to avoid the conceptual and empirical difficulties associated with measuring income. Households that qualify for the program are assured of having benefits for three years; at that point a new measurement is taken to determine whether they will continue to receive benefits.[2]

The program has three closely associated and complementary components: nutrition, education, and health. The amount of benefits received depends on household composition (number of members as well as age and gender of each) and on the fulfillment of a set of conditions for each component.

The nutrition component is a mix of cash and in-kind benefits. All households in the program receive the same monthly cash stipend, regardless of their demographic composition. In addition, pregnant or nursing women, infants between four months and two years of age, and undernourished children between three and five years of age receive an appropriate in-kind nutritional supplement that provides on average 20 percent of the kilocalories and 100 percent of the micronutrients that they require.[3] Households can receive their cash transfers and nutritional supplements only if they attend a health clinic regularly. Cash transfers are indexed to the consumer price index (CPI) to protect their purchasing power, and they are delivered to the mother or, in her absence, to the person responsible for seeing that the children in the household are fed and sent to school. Households can freely dispose of their cash at any store to purchase food or any other items; they also can acquire productive assets or save money for the future.

The health component is delivered when households visit the health clinics to qualify for the cash transfer associated with the nutritional component. The frequency of visits depends on household composition, and with the exception of pregnant and nursing women, it decreases as members grow older. At health clinics two interventions take place. First, mothers are given a series of talks that deliver information on various health and nutrition topics, including reproductive health; teenagers also must attend talks related to reproductive health and to drug addiction.

---

1. Among these are age, gender, and education of each member of the household; whether the housing unit has access to electricity and tap water; and whether it has assets like radio, television, and bicycles. The point system is based on the discriminant analysis statistical technique; see Gómez de León (1998).

2. Incentives to remain or abandon the program are not addressed here; see chapter 5.

3. Nutritional supplements for infants start after four months to promote breast-feeding of newborns.

Second, a protocol of basic health interventions is followed that consists, among other things, of anthropometric measurements of children, vaccinations, and early prevention and treatment of diarrhea, respiratory infections, tuberculosis, high blood pressure, diabetes, and cervical/uterine cancer. Nutritional supplements are distributed at health clinics.

The education component consists of three elements. First, all girls and boys who attend school for 85 percent or more of school days each month from the third grade of primary school through the end of high school receive a monthly cash transfer (or scholarship) for ten months of each year. Cash transfers increase with each school year, and after secondary school they are larger for girls than for boys because drop-out rates are higher for girls beginning at approximately that stage. Second, all students who finish high school receive an additional one-time cash transfer. Third, subsidies are given for school supplies. At the primary level they are given in two installments, one at the beginning of the year upon enrollment and one in the middle of the school year. At the secondary and high school level there is a single payment at the beginning of the year upon enrollment. Subsidies are paid in cash; as with nutritional cash transfers, they are indexed to the CPI and can be freely disposed of by households. Figure 2-1 shows how the cash transfers for the education component increase with gender and school age and matches that information with the mid-1990s figures for school attendance by poor children.

Three comments concerning these benefits are in order. First, all the cash and in-kind components of the program add up to an average transfer of US$35 per month, approximately 25 percent of average poor rural household income in the absence of the program and between 15 to 20 percent of poor urban household income. Of that amount, cash transfers from the education component represent about 50 percent; cash transfers from the nutritional component, 36 percent; in-kind food supplements, approximately 4 percent; and medicines and other services provided at health clinics, 10 percent. Thus, more than 85 percent of the benefits of the program are in cash. Cash transfers for the nutrition and education component are paid jointly once every two months.[4]

Second, the bulk of the income transfers follow the family's life cycle, as illustrated in figure 2-2, where total cash transfers are mapped as a function of years of marital union for a typical household. The lower

---

4. Author's calculations based on program data provided by the Coordinación Nacional del Programa de Desarollo Humano Oportunidades (National Coordinating Agency for the Human Development Program Oportunidades).

Figure 2-1. *School Attendance and Education Grants*

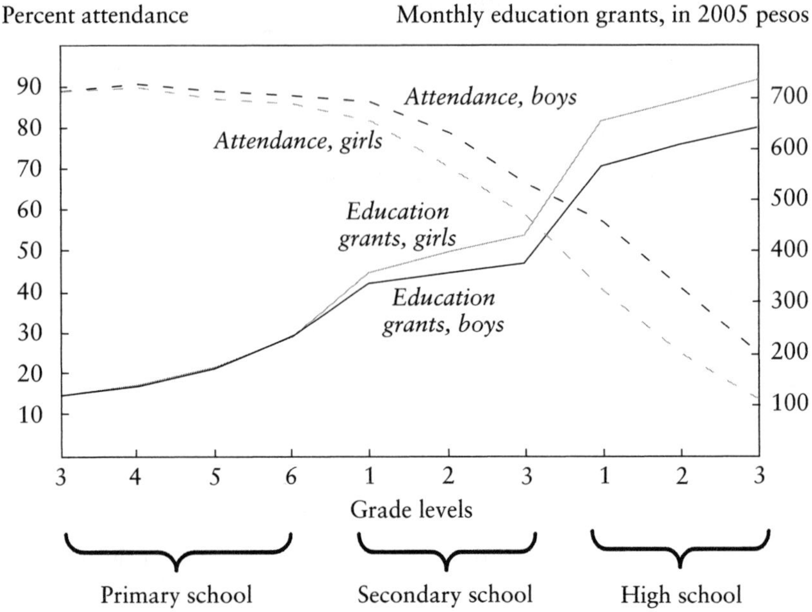

Percent attendance   Monthly education grants, in 2005 pesos

Source: Author's update of Levy and Rodriguez (2004) with data from the National Coordinating Agency for the Human Development Program Oportunidades.

bound on the transfer is the nutritional component (or food subsidy), received by all families regardless of their size; this is equal to approximately US$15 per month. Total cash transfers increase with the number of children in school and with the increase in school grade level, as the educational transfer is added to the nutritional transfer. That increase implies that even though the average cash transfer for all families is US$35 a month, it is substantially higher for families with children in school. There is, however, an upper bound on total cash transfers of approximately US$153 per month regardless of the number of children or school attendance, set to avoid generating incentives for couples to have large families.[5] Note that more than 50 percent of program benefits are temporary, in order to avoid encouraging permanent dependence on the program.

Third, with the exception of the free nutritional supplements, Progresa-Oportunidades offers no food subsidies. Households face market prices

5. The impact of the program on fertility is discussed in chapter 3.

Figure 2-2. *Monthly Household Monetary Transfers*

Monthly transfers, 2005 pesos

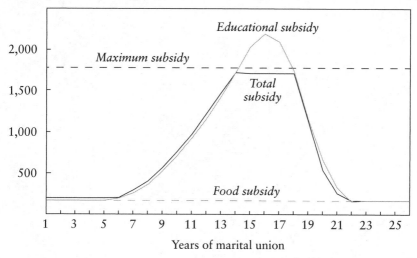

Source: Author's update of Levy and Rodriguez (2004) with data from the National Coordinating Agency for the Human Development Program Oportunidades.

for all food or nonfood items that they purchase. As elaborated on in chapter 4, generalized food subsidies for bread and tortillas have been fully phased out: subsidies for food items in rural public stores have diminished rapidly and are not significant. With the exception of school breakfasts, the program has substituted monetary income transfers for practically all food subsidies.

The Scope of Progresa-Oportunidades

From its introduction in August 1997 through December 2005, Progresa-Oportunidades grew rapidly; it is now the largest single poverty alleviation program in Mexico's history. To quantify the scope of the program, aggregate figures on household coverage, geographical reach, benefits extended, and budgetary resources are provided in tables 2-1 through 2-5.

Table 2-1 shows coverage of households, states, municipalities, and localities for the first nine years of program operation. Given that poor households have 4.8 members on average, at the end of 2005 the program covered 24.06 million people, or 23.8 percent of Mexico's population,

Table 2-1. *Indicators of Progresa-Oportunidades Coverage, 1997–2005*
Number covered

Participants	1997	1998	1999	2000	2001	2002	2003	2004	2005
Beneficiary families									
(thousands)	300.7	1,595.6	2,306.3	2,476.4	3,116	4,240	4,184.4	5,000	5,000
States	12	30	31	31	31	31	31	31	31
Municipalities	357	1,750	2,155	2,166	2,310	2,354	2,360	2,429	2,435
Localities	6,344	40,711	53,152	53,232	67,539	70,520	70,436	82,973	86,091

Source: Author's update of Levy and Rodríguez (2004) with data from the National Coordinating Agency for the Human Development Program Oportunidades.

which was estimated at 103 million in 2005.[6] The number of people covered is slightly larger than the number of people living in extreme poverty
in the country in 2004, the latest year for which poverty statistics were
gathered.[7] (Exclusion and inclusion errors are discussed in chapter 3.)

Data on the geographical distribution of beneficiary households shows
that Progresa-Oportunidades has expanded in line with the geographical
distribution of poverty. The six states that account for the greatest share of
poverty in Mexico (Chiapas, Mexico State, Puebla, Veracruz, Oaxaca, and
Guerrero), with 48.2 percent of the total, are home to 53.6 percent of program households. The six states with the smallest share (Baja California,
Baja California Sur, Aguascalientes, Colima, Quintana Roo, and Nayarit),
at 2.95 percent, are home to 3.35 percent of program households.[8]

Since both the absolute number of people living in poverty and the
depth and severity of poverty were greater in rural than in urban areas,
the expansion strategy followed initially gave preference to rural areas
and, within rural areas, to more highly marginalized communities. Table
2-2 shows how the program gradually expanded from the smallest and
most marginalized rural localities into relatively less marginalized and
larger localities. Large urban areas were the last to be covered, because of
the reasons given and also because those areas could have presented
larger operational and political risks—in particular, program capture by
relatively better-off urban dwellers and greater difficulty in replacing the
targeted milk and tortilla programs, which were substantially more
prevalent there than in rural areas.

Table 2-3 shows figures for nutrition, health, and education benefits.
Three observations may be made. First, at the end of 2005 Progresa-
Oportunidades was providing nutritional assistance to 2.1 million children

6. Figures for household size are from the Coordinación Nacional del Programa de
Desarrollo Humano Oportunidades. Those for national population in 2005 are from the
Instituto Nacional de Estadistica, Geografia, e Informatica (National Institute of Statistics,
Geography, and Information Technology).

7. The Technical Committee for the Measurement of Poverty (an independent group of
academic researchers sponsored by the Ministry of Social Development) has elaborated
three complementary definitions of "poverty line": a food poverty line, a capabilities
poverty line, and an asset poverty line. In 2004 the head-count ratios for each of the lines
were 15.8 percent, 21.1 percent, and 44.1 percent, respectively. The targeting system for
Progresa-Oportunidades is based on the capabilities poverty line, implying that in 2005
approximately 21 percent of the population was living in poverty, according to this definition. See Secretaría de Desarrollo Social (2005).

8. Levy and Rodriguez (2004, table 21). The contribution of each state to national
poverty is derived from an index based on the severity of poverty.

Table 2-2. Coverage of Localities during Expansion of Progresa-Oportunidades, 1997–2005
Number covered

Degree of marginalization of locality	Number of inhabitants of locality	Total localities	1997	1998	1999	2000	2001	2002	2003	2004	2005
High—very high	499 or less	77,371	4,720	30,600	35,512	38,009	48,101	49,942	49,861	50,810	52,593
	500 to 2,499	9,081	1,273	6,808	6,284	6,578	6,731	8,698	8,715	8,795	8,841
	2,500 or more	786	87	530	365	380	516	763	763	771	774
Moderate	499 or less	10,910	110	2,164	3,690	4,761	6,575	5,250	5,236	6,396	6,703
	500 to 2,499	3,377	78	935	2,169	2,582	3,006	2,024	2,054	2,944	3,001
	2,500 or more	873	28	293	210	296	497	784	790	851	865
Low—very low	499 or less	6,504	20	254	127	185	263	1,079	1,080	2,074	2,228
	500 to 2,499	1,597	9	130	158	211	257	549	582	1,400	1,465
	2,500 or more	1,383	45	343	63	76	1,069	1,047	1,068	1,055	1,346
No index available	499 or less	89,012	0	0	131	130	499	384	353	7,573	8,183
	500 to 2,499	1	0	0	10	24	17	0	0	88	89
	2,500 or more	n.a.[a]	0	0	0	0	2	0	0	3	3
Total		200,895	6,370	42,057	48,719	53,232	67,533	70,520	70,502	82,973	86,091

Source: Author's update of Levy and Rodríguez (2004) with data from the National Coordinating Agency for the Human Development Program Oportunidades.

a. n.a. = not available.

Table 2-3. *Coverage of Progresa-Oportunidades Benefits, 1997–2005*

Benefit	1997	1998	1999	2000	2001	2002	2003	2004	2005
Nutrition									
Nutritional supplements distributed									
(millions of doses)	5.0	254.1	543.8	555.7	665.3	566.4	529.2	523.6	561.3
To children under five	2.7	153.1	372.8	386.7	494.5	410.6	390.3	391.2	416.5
To pregnant and nursing mothers	2.3	101.0	171.0	169.0	170.8	155.8	138.9	132.4	144.7
Health care									
Average number of consultations pro-									
vided per month (thousands)	n.a.[a]	435.0	1,359.8	1,624.8	1836.4	2,295.8	2,661.5	2,903.1	3,342.9
Training courses provided in health,									
nutrition, and hygiene (thousands)	n.a.[a]	1,637.1	2,867.5	2,004.4	2,088.7	2,266.9	2,604.0	3,073.0	3,103.2
Education									
Education grants provided (thousands)	101.1	1,299.0	2,192.6	2,485.3	3,325.5	4,361.2	4,603.1	5,100.3	5,298.8
Packages of school supplies distributed									
(thousands)	72.6	684.9	1,314.5	1,249.5	1,498.5	1,640.0	1,738.3	1,809.6	1,846.6

Source: Author's update of Levy and Rodriguez (2004) with data from the National Coordinating Agency for the Human Development Program Oportunidades.

a. n.a. = not available.

Table 2-4. *Scope of Progresa-Oportunidades Benefits, 1997–2005*

Benefit	July 1997– December 2000	January 2001– December 2002	January 2003– December 2005
Nutrition	Nutritional supplements	Same	Improved formula for supplements
Health care	Preventive health interventions Health talks	Expanded health topics for mothers and youngsters	Same
Education	School supplies Education grants until secondary school	Education grants until high school	Additional cash transfers on completion of high school

Source: Author's compilation.

under age five and close to 1 million women (figures were calculated on the basis of daily administration of nutritional supplements to children between four months and two years of age and up to age five in cases of malnutrition, to pregnant women over a period of seven months, and to nursing mothers for one year). Second, given an average of 7.8 medical consultations per family per year, during 2005 a total of 42.5 million medical consultations took place under the program. Third, 5.3 million children and young people between the third grade of primary school and high school were receiving education grants. The national estimated school population within this age range is 28.4 million, implying that 18.7 percent of all children in Mexico in those grades were attending school on a program education grant. To put those figures into perspective, in 1994 the federal government financed a total of 648,000 education grants, of which nearly 99 percent were for primary school under the Children in Solidarity Program. These figures indicate that the number of children and young people with education grants increased more than eightfold between 1994 and 2005.[9]

It should be noted that not all benefits were incorporated into the program from the beginning. Table 2-4 shows that they have increased in scope over time or that their content has been modified (as is the case with nutritional supplements). For the most part, modifications have been based on the results of the evaluation studies discussed in the next chapter.

Finally, table 2-5, which shows the budgetary resources allocated to

9. Levy and Rodriguez (2004).

Table 2-5. *Progresa-Oportunidades Budget, 1997–2005*
Millions of 2005 pesos, unless otherwise noted

	1997	1998	1999	2000	2001	2002	2003	2004	2005	2005 (millions of US$)
Food										
Nutritional supplements	46.3	1,203.9	940.9	1,073.2	1,123.9	1,763.6	933.2	642.0	665.7	62.2
Food transfers	121.9	1,283.4	3,774.9	4,710.6	5,208.1	6,823.8	8,081.2	8,715.7	9,479.2	885.9
Health	95.2	1,112.6	710.0	809.7	1,223.9	1,848.3	2,010.1	2,734.3	3,162.7	295.6
Education (grants and school supplies)	164.8	1,142.2	3,537.3	5,089.9	6,752.9	9,524.1	11,974.4	12,952.1	15,137.9	1,414.8
Operating expenses	448.2	774.2	629.1	506.6	895.2	1,219.3	1,504.4	1,631.2	1,706.1	159.4
Operating expenses as a percentage of total spending	0.51	0.14	0.06	0.04	0.06	0.06	0.06	0.06	0.05	0.05
Total	876.4	5,516.3	9,592.2	12,190	15,204	21,179.1	24,503.3	26,675.3	30,151.2	2,817.9

Source: Author's update of Levy and Rodríguez (2004) with data from the Ministry of Finance.

the program during the period under discussion, elicits two observations. (To facilitate comparisons, figures for 2005 are also expressed in U.S. dollars in the last column.) First, program expenditures rose substantially. Second, operating expenses stabilized at around 6 percent of the total budget, except during the first year, when many of the initial outlays were made. Accordingly, of every fiscal peso earmarked for the program, a full ninety-four centavos represent a direct benefit to families; of that amount, eighty-two centavos are a direct monetary transfer and twelve centavos are in-kind transfers, mainly for nutritional supplements. Note that these figures do not include the costs of health and education provision, which are part of the normal budget of the ministries of health and education, respectively.

In 2005 Progresa-Oportunidades made direct monetary transfers to 5 million families, amounting to close to 24,617 million pesos (US$2.30 billion), and provided in-kind benefits worth 3,828 million pesos (or US$357 million). This represents direct monetary assistance of 4,923 pesos in cash (US$460) and 765 pesos in kind (US$71.40) per family per year, or 474 pesos (US$44.30) per family per month. These transfers are second in size only to those associated with social security pensions.[10]

10. Author's calculations based on data in tables 2-1 and 2-5.

CHAPTER THREE

Program
Results

The analytical and operational observations made in chapter 1 suggest that replacing in-kind income transfers with cash and imposing explicit conditions for receipt on beneficiary households would increase their income and human capital more effectively than had the set of programs existing in Mexico in the mid-1990s. There was, however, no empirical evidence to demonstrate that that would in fact be the case. There were programs, both in Mexico and abroad, that had tied together nutrition and food interventions or food and schooling interventions; there also were programs in which cash transfers were carried out on a large scale, even in rural areas.[1]

Nonetheless, Progresa-Oportunidades was uncommon, perhaps novel, for seven reasons: first, it tied three interventions together; second, it imposed explicit conditions; third, it used new targeting methods; fourth, it delivered benefits to mothers; fifth, it replaced in-kind with cash subsidies; sixth, it introduced a life-cycle approach; and seventh, critically, it introduced all these elements at the same time.

1. In particular, an underestimated precedent for Progresa-Oportunidades was a program launched in 1994 in the context of Mexico's entry into the North American Free Trade Agreement that replaced protection for maize producers in Mexico with cash transfers; see Levy and van Wijnbergen (1992, 1994, and 1995). Human capital considerations aside, the program showed that it was feasible to deliver cash transfers in small and remote rural areas.

The program's designers were aware that this approach was a significant departure from the norm, certainly for poverty policy in Mexico and probably by international standards as well. It was therefore essential, from the beginning, to determine whether the underlying hypotheses were correct. That was done in two distinct stages: program design and program scale-up. The first stage sought simply to demonstrate that a program with these features could operate; the second, more important stage sought to demonstrate that it was better than the programs that it replaced.

This chapter places evaluation of Progresa-Oportunidades in the context of its overall design and summarizes its results. It briefly describes the simpler but initially more critical first stage described above—for the obvious reason that the second stage would never have occurred if major problems were observed in the first—and presents some general observations about the relationship between evaluation and program design. It then discusses the main results of the evaluations of the program and summarizes program results.

Testing the Operational Hypothesis

In March 1995, for the first time, Finance Ministry officials proposed to President Ernesto Zedillo and his Cabinet that the government replace in-kind distributions of milk and tortillas and price subsidies for bread and tortillas with targeted cash transfers for mothers, contingent on household members' regular attendance at health clinics (the proposal to expand transfers and condition them on school attendance was added in 1996). The objective was to have a single comprehensive program to transfer income to all poor households, whether urban or rural. At the time, that was a fairly novel proposition, and it was met with justifiable skepticism by some Cabinet members. Three questions arose:

—Would the substitution of cash for in-kind transfers lead to less spending on food and more on goods like cigarettes and alcohol?

—Would giving cash to mothers lead to family disruption and potentially to family violence?

—Was making cash transfers contingent on compliance with requirements operationally feasible?

To answer those questions, the Finance Ministry implemented a pilot project in the state of Campeche involving 31,000 households and commissioned an external evaluation.[2] On one hand, the evaluation allowed the officials to reject the idea that use of cash transfers would lead to inappropriate use of the funds and to family disruption. A large majority of households preferred cash to in-kind subsidies and actually valued the link to health services; furthermore, cash transfers did not diminish households' food consumption, particularly of tortillas. On the other hand, the evaluation pointed out that before program scale-up could be contemplated, targeting and selection methods had to be substantially revised and more and better data collected.[3] In addition, the pilot project operated on a completely ad hoc basis, hiring health personnel under temporary contracts and working in premises that were not entirely suitable. A different administrative set-up would be needed for a large-scale effort.

The pilot project was essential for three reasons. First, it provided assurance to the government that the change being contemplated was not unduly risky, given its potential benefits. Second, it made clear that none of the existing federal government agencies or ministries had any incentive to coordinate a much larger-scale operation, forcing program designers to deal explicitly with that issue. And third, it established a decision-making mechanism whereby the results of external evaluations, although perhaps not decisive, would nevertheless be seriously weighed in conjunction with other considerations. Learning from the pilot project and having time to adapt the program accordingly were instrumental in solving many unexpected operational issues.[4] These factors contributed to the elaboration of a more solid proposal prior to program scale-up, a task that took most of 1996.

2. The pilot project was unannounced and implemented in Campeche, which is relatively far from Mexico City, in order not to attract too much political attention. Finance Ministry officials fortunately had the cooperation of a few high-level officials from the Ministry of Social Development, which, at that time, was not in favor of the new approach. The evaluation was performed by the Instituto Tecnológico Autónomo de México, a well-known university in Mexico City, and by the Ministry of the Comptrollership; see Secretaría de la Contraloría y Desarrollo Administrativo (1996), and De Alba, Alagon, and Villa (1997).

3. In the course of 1996, when adding school scholarships was being contemplated, it also was clear that more work would be needed to calculate the value of the scholarships on the basis of the opportunity costs of children's time; this component of Progresa-Oportunidades was not part of the Campeche pilot project.

4. The pilot project operated in medium-sized urban localities, where payments to households were made with an electronic card; in remote rural communities that was not feasible and alternative methods had to be developed.

Evaluation and Program Design

Results of the evaluation of the pilot program were limited. First, there was little time to measure any lasting effects on poor households' human capital; second, the Campeche program did not incorporate the effects of schooling. Thus, although encouraging, the results were insufficient to fully convince all the decisionmakers involved of the benefits of the new approach, and many doubts remained. Because a larger-scale effort was being considered, it was clear that systematic evaluation efforts needed to be incorporated into the program.[5] Further, if one of the shortcomings of previous efforts was that systematic evaluations were lacking, then it was unreasonable for Progresa-Oportunidades not to have them from the start. Three factors played a central role at this stage.

First, as elaborated on in the next chapter, the program began under difficult macroeconomic circumstances. There was both a tight fiscal situation and substantial uncertainty, for international and domestic reasons (changes in world oil prices and in the composition of Congress). Budget projections varied significantly, and it was unclear at the time how many households the program would be able to cover or how fast it would be able to grow. Second, the process of carrying out the household and locality surveys, analyzing the data, applying the targeting system, and setting up reporting procedures in clinics and schools in order to certify that participants had met program requirements would be gradual. Therefore, operational and budgetary reasons indicated that full coverage of the program's target population from the start would not be possible; some poor families would not receive benefits for some time. Third, it was calculated that the data-gathering effort that was being carried out for program operations (particularly for targeting localities and households) could be extended, with little additional cost and potentially large benefits, to include data to be used for program evaluation.

These factors complemented each other and contributed to program evaluation efforts. Evaluation, in turn, was needed in two separate dimensions: operations and results. Otherwise it would be impossible, if

5. Evaluation was incorporated into the program's design for the most part because of the designers' central preoccupation with results and program survival and because of the constant pressure of critics who saw, at that time, a major (and dangerous) departure from Mexico's traditional social policy. Program designers were very aware of the novelty and the risks involved, but they were hardly aware that, ex post, this feature of the program would be the center of so much attention.

Progresa-Oportunidades was not working, to determine whether that was the result of faulty design or deficient operation. If, for example, the program had no impact on school enrollment, empirical evidence was needed to evaluate whether it was because households were not responding to the incentive system or because teachers were not reporting attendance; similarly, if the program had no impact on nutrition, it was important to see whether it was because the nutritional supplements were faulty or because clinics were not distributing them to households. These two dimensions of evaluation were started at the same time over the course of 1997 and 1998.

Before presenting the results, it is useful to offer observations in five areas of interest: type of analysis required; data used in quantitative evaluations; methods used in quantitative evaluations; integrated nature of the program; and credibility of the results.

—*Type of analysis required.* To obtain a more rounded and balanced perspective of the program, particularly in the case of impact evaluations, both quantitative and qualitative analyses were performed. The former provides evidence on variables amenable to measurement and systematic statistical analysis; the latter provides evidence of attitudes, perceptions, and impacts derived from interviews, focus groups, and other methods of analysis. Both types are useful and contribute to understanding the full dimensions of such a complex program; furthermore, some policymakers may rely more on a given set of indicators and others on a different set.

—*Data used in quantitative impact evaluations.* To a large extent, the econometric techniques applied take advantage of the gradual growth in program coverage. In particular, since some localities and families were incorporated into Progresa-Oportunidades earlier and some later, the first set of localities and families could be considered subject to the effects of the program and the second set representative of what happens in the absence of the program (until they are incorporated); in other terms, the first set would be the treatment group and the second the control group.

If both sets of localities and households are chosen randomly and if repeated observations of the same variables are collected for both sets to obtain data before and after program implementation, then econometric techniques can be applied to the resulting databases to obtain numerical estimates of program impacts. That was in fact done. Between October 1997 and November 1999, a total of 24,000 families in 506 localities were interviewed regularly. Of those localities, 320 that were incorporated in the program as of October 1997 were in the initial treatment group and 186 were in the control group, until they were incorporated in the program in late 1999 (within each locality, all households that were eligible for the program were incorporated at the same time). These procedures have been continued and repeated observations collected on households and localities incorporated "earlier" and "later" through different stages of program scale-up.[6] The information collected was complemented with administrative records from health clinics and schools in both sets of localities. Altogether, the data have permitted officials to measure the impact of the program on a large number of variables of interest, as summarized below.

Note that to the extent that data for program operations were gathered at the same time as data for evaluation, the speed of implementation was not affected by the needs of the evaluation effort. The key was incorporating evaluation as part of program design and not as an afterthought. Otherwise, evaluation could have delayed program scale-up.

—*Methods used in quantitative evaluations.* In general, the effect of the program on a given variable is determined by the difference between the mean value of that variable in the treatment group and its mean value in the control group. To obtain as accurate an estimate as possible, the mean values of variables are obtained using regression methods, whereby other variables are incorporated to try to control for additional factors that might also have an effect on the variable of interest. Put differently, an attempt is made to isolate to the extent possible the pure effects of the program, since the control factors are included in the regressions for both treatment and control groups; in principle, the only observable difference between the groups is the effect of the program. If the mean values of the variable of interest in both treatment and control groups are statistically different, the difference is interpreted as the effect of the program on that variable (since, again, nothing else could, in principle, have generated that difference).

Techniques for measuring and comparing the mean values of variables have varied in the many evaluations performed so far. The most common, however, has been the double difference technique. To facilitate the interpretation of results obtained by this technique, figure 3-1 presents a hopefully intuitive example.[7] On the horizontal axis, T refers to the

6. Levy and Rodriguez (2004). When all eligible households are incorporated, the comparison between treatment and control groups can no longer be carried out and different econometric techniques are required for quantitative impact evaluation.

7. See Levy and Rodriguez (2004, appendix 2) and Skoufias (2005, chapter 3), for a presentation of the evaluation problem in Progresa-Oportunidades; the references contained in both have the relevant background material. The discussion in Skoufias covers many of the technical issues in evaluation very well.

Figure 3-1. *Double Difference Estimation*

Variable of interest

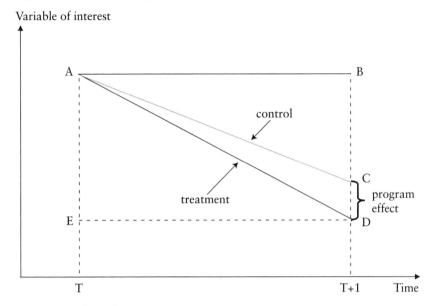

Source: Author's illustration.

period before the program, and T+ 1 to the period after (the time elapsed can be any number of months or even years). The vertical axis measures the value of the variable of interest (say, the rate of infant mortality, consumption of meat, years of schooling, number of visits to a health clinic, and so on). In the two localities at date T, one in the program and the other not, the variable of interest is measured (A). The same measurement is performed in both localities at date T+1, and the results are recorded: in the treatment locality the variable is now D, and in the control locality it is C.

A simple comparison of the before-and-after values looking only at the treatment locality indicates that the effect of the program on the variable of interest was the distance BD (point A and B have the same value). But that is not really the case. The point here is that even in the absence of the program, that variable would have changed for other reasons (for example, infant mortality already was on a downward trend as a result of other programs). That can be seen by looking at what happened in the control locality, where there was no program. There the variable of interest changed from B to C. Thus, the true program effect is only CD, the difference in the variable of interest in the treatment group, BD, minus the difference in the variable of interest in the control group, BC. Hence the term "difference in difference," or "double difference." (In the example the variable of interest had the same value in both localities before the program started, at A; that need not be the case, and the technique produces the same results even if the variable of interest started with different values.) It is important to note that the technique is reliable because households measured in the treatment locality before and after the program are the same households, as is the case with the households in the control locality (that is, the data used in the analysis are a panel data set). It is also important to note that localities must be chosen randomly for each of the two sets before the start of the program; thus the treatment locality could have been the control locality or vice versa.[8]

At this point it is necessary to discuss two complications. First, as program coverage expands, control localities diminish; eventually all localities are in the treatment group. That modifies the nature of possible comparisons, which now must be made between households that received treatment earlier and those that received it later. In this case, what is measured are the different effects of treatment at two time periods (or lengths of program exposure); the measurement is not a zero-one comparison of receiving or not receiving treatment.

The second complication relates to the interaction between targeting methods and randomization. As described above, in the initial stages of the program, rural localities were randomly selected to be in or out of the program, and within each locality exhaustive household surveys were conducted to gather the information necessary for the point system of targeting households. But in some urban areas that was not the case, as it was no longer feasible to visit and gather data for all households in all localities. Hence, a new method based on the preliminary self-selection of families into the program was introduced. In urban areas where it was infeasible to visit all households, program modules were set up, and families could voluntarily come to the module and request incorporation into the program. At this module a short survey would be completed, followed by a longer survey applied directly at the household. With these

---

8. Behrman and Todd (1999a, 1999b) elaborate on the importance of randomness for the validity of the results. Not all reports used double difference estimators; some used a cross-sectional difference operator, which does not control properly for initial differences in the mean values of the variable of interest in the control and treatment groups; Skoufias (2005, chapter 3) discusses this in detail.

data, the point system was then applied to determine households' eligibility for the program.

The use of different targeting methods in some urban areas and the gradual exhaustion of control localities in rural areas (and, eventually, in urban ones), modifies the nature of the evaluation. On one hand, the selection process is no longer random; on the other, the control group may not be directly observed and measured. As a result, first, for some purposes the decision of a household to participate in the program or not must be taken into account (for example, whether the household knew about the program and whether the household decided to apply), requiring a behavioral model of participation to be incorporated into the evaluation analysis. Second, different statistical techniques are required to construct the control group. In particular, to make a comparison between treatment and nontreatment groups, quasi-experimental design methods are used, whereby the control group (or the counterfactual) is, so to speak, artificially constructed.

Progresa-Oportunidades started in more remote and smaller rural communities, gradually scaled up into larger rural and semi-urban localities, and entered larger urban areas last. As a result, most of the earlier evaluations, particularly in rural areas, identified the with-and-without effects of the program (by using double difference or similar techniques). At the same time, the underlying randomization used to select localities implied that it was not necessary to model households' program participation decisions. As time has elapsed and more localities have been incorporated, more recent evaluations in rural areas present the results of being in the program earlier or later (mostly by using double difference techniques). In some cases, matching methods are used to construct a control group to present with-and-without program results.[9] In general, a household's decision to participate in the program or not is not modeled. Evaluations in urban areas, on the other hand, at times model that decision as part of the analysis in order to correct for the nonrandomness of the selection process (who does or does not go into the incorporation module), and they may also use matching methods to construct a control group. In interpreting the program's results, it is important to keep these distinctions in mind: it is not the same, for example, to compare the impact of the program on rural families incorporated in 1997 with its

---

9. In these methods, the control group is not directly observed and measured. Rather, it is constructed using data from other groups that have statistically similar characteristics.

impact on urban families incorporated in 2004. Variations may be due to inherent urban-rural differences, to differences in the short- and medium-term effects of the program, or to other factors affecting household program participation.

More generally, all possible evaluation outcomes can be organized in a two-dimensional matrix. One dimension corresponds to short- and medium-run results for rural and urban localities (somewhat arbitrarily, "short term" refers to impacts in the first three years of program exposure and "medium term" to impacts between four and six years); the second dimension corresponds to the variable that is being evaluated (infant mortality, fertility, high school enrollment, and so on). Each cell of the matrix refers to the impact on a variable in a given area over a certain time period. At the same time, the results of a given evaluation contained in any one cell might result from a qualitative or quantitative analysis (there might be more than one evaluation in a given cell). Last, the econometric technique used for each evaluation might vary depending on the nature of the control group, data availability, and the randomness of the selection process.

Progresa's initial evaluations concern short-run impacts on standard health, consumption, nutrition, and schooling variables in rural households, as well as on the effectiveness of the targeting methods. Gradually, evaluations have produced medium-term results for rural areas and short-run results for urban areas; eventually medium-term results for urban areas will become available as well. The number of variables of interest also has expanded, and more recent analysis looks at health variables that were not looked at before (for example, impact on incidence of diabetes), schooling variables (for example, impact on performance), or altogether new issues that had not been explored (for example, impact on saving and investing in productive projects). Mirroring that evolution, differences in effects in households that entered the treatment group earlier and those that entered later are being obtained; matching methods are being used to construct counterfactuals for treatment and nontreatment households; and models of household participation are being incorporated in the analysis. The point here is that evaluation of Progresa-Oportunidades is a process guided by the program's evolution, with an enlarging set of questions and a broader use of statistical techniques. Two consequences follow: first, most obviously, outcomes are very rich. Second, and more important, making a definitive assessment of the program may be premature, to the extent that new results are still being produced.

—*Integrated nature of the program.* It is not possible in the evaluations to identify the impact of program components separately. In accordance with the original program design, those effects are closely interlinked. It is not correct to conclude, for example, that the program's impact on school enrollment derives from the education transfers or to attribute the impact on nutrition to the nutritional supplements. School enrollment might also have been affected by higher family income from the food transfers, and improved nutrition might result from visits to the health centers. Evaluation can assess only the impact of the program overall. To measure the impact of the individual components, it would have been necessary to vary the components (type and level) in different communities. However, that option, which was suggested by the evaluators as the program was being launched in 1997, was ruled out by program officials.

—*Credibility of the results.* There always is a subjective element in assessing credibility, but efforts need to be made to reduce any doubts to the minimum possible. In the case of Progresa-Oportunidades, the efforts consisted of making the databases available to many researchers, so that results could, in principle, be replicated; relying on a mix of national and international academic researchers and domestic and foreign institutions to perform evaluations; and placing no restrictions on researchers with regard to divulging their results.

In particular, during the first three years of the program, the International Food Policy Research Institute (IFPRI) was hired by the Mexican government to perform an important part of the evaluation. IFPRI in turn relied on a team of outside and in-house professionals, including well-known academics from American universities. The results of the IFPRI evaluations, which correspond mostly to short-run impacts in rural areas, are summarized in Skoufias (2005). The Mexican government also hired Mexican researchers and academic institutions that have made equally valuable contributions to program evaluation, notably the Instituto Nacional de Salud Pública (INSP) (National Institute of Public Health) and the Centro de Investigacion y Estudios Superiores en Antropología Social (CIESAS) (Center for Research and Advanced Studies in Social Anthropology). The results of their evaluations and those of IFPRI are summarized in Levy and Rodriguez (2004), as well as the results of some short-run evaluations for urban areas up to 2003. The Mexican government continued to sponsor evaluations over 2004 and 2005. Studies corresponding to more recent results are collected in Oportunidades (2005a,

2005b, 2005c, 2005d, and 2005e); they contain short-run impacts for urban areas and medium-term impacts for rural areas and results for some dimensions of the program not previously studied. These, as well as the previous results, are all reviewed here. As of June 2006, additional evaluations commissioned by the Mexican government of other program impacts were not yet available. In addition, the increasing visibility of Progresa-Oportunidades and the wealth of data collected and made available have attracted other national and international researchers from universities, international development banks, and policy-oriented research institutions; some of these evaluations and research papers also are available and reviewed here. All this work has benefited the program and contributed to the credibility of the evaluation results. It could be said that a decade ago, program designers and administrators never expected such a response, although, ex post, all are pleasantly surprised.

Impact Evaluation: Consumption and Saving and Investment

This section reviews the impact of Progresa-Oportunidades on households' income and consumption, with emphasis on food consumption. It also discusses the extent to which program income transfers have been saved or invested in productive projects.

Consumption

Progresa-Oportunidades was designed, in principle, to replace other food subsidy programs. But as mentioned, food subsidy programs had very little coverage in rural areas. To that extent, Progresa-Oportunidades was not so much substituting one form of income transfer for another as actually increasing households' net income. An important question therefore arose regarding the impact of the additional income on consumption, particularly food consumption. In the case of rural households, Hoddinott, Skoufias and Washburn (2000) found that average consumption expenditures increased by almost 15 percent between March 1998 and November 1999; of that increase, 72 percent went to food. Per capita food consumption in program households rose by 10.6 percent. Among poorer families, food consumption rose by 13.5 percent in comparison with consumption in nonprogram families. The increase was concentrated in two areas: fruits and vegetables (16 percent) and food items of animal origin (30 percent); in particular, consumption of poultry was up 19 percent and that of beef and pork was up 20 percent. By November 1999, the caloric intake of program households had risen almost 8 percent compared with that of nonprogram families. Together these results indicate that program families not only consumed more food, but that they had a more balanced and better-quality diet. An important question was whether nutritional supplements would replace spending on food; the analysis revealed that that was not the case. With respect to nonfood consumption, program families showed higher per capita spending due mainly to lower school-related costs, although a higher percentage of nonfood spending went toward clothing and shoes for children than before.

The qualitative evaluation presented in Escobar and González de la Rocha (2003) found that schoolchildren were eating better and more frequent breakfasts, especially at home.[10] Teachers noticed that children had new shoes and clothing and were better fed, and there were no reports of widespread use of money for "men's vices" (for example, drinking and smoking). At the same time, better access to health services meant healthier household members and lower medical costs. Last, program households were found to have made more improvements to their homes than nonprogram families.

Angelucci, Attanasio, and Shaw (2004) studied the impact of Progresa-Oportunidades on consumption of urban households incorporated in the program in 2003. Total consumption by beneficiary households increased by 6 percent, with food consumption rising by 10 percent. The authors found that "among food items, consumption of proteins and fruits and vegetables increased the most."[11] The authors consider their results to be lower-bound estimates of the impact of the program; they also note that their results contradict Engel's Law (which states that when a family's income increases, the proportion of money that it spends on food decreases) and speculate that that might be a short-run result.[12]

An important question was whether the income transfers from Progresa-Oportunidades would generate inflationary pressures in small rural communities, where the supply of food could be inelastic (an argument made at times by proponents of public food stores or in-kind distribution of

10. The evaluation was based on a study of six semi-urban communities (between 2,500 and 50,000 inhabitants) that were incorporated into the program in September 2001.

11. Angelucci, Attanasio, and Shaw (2004, p. 56); author's translation.

12. This might not be so surprising. Much earlier work by Lustig, using the 1977 *National Household Income-Expenditure Survey* published by the National Institute of Statistics, found an income food elasticity greater than one in thirteen of eighteen regions of Mexico; see Lustig (1984).

food items; see Davila and Levy 2004). The work by Hoddinott, Skoufias and Washburn (2000) found that not to be the case. More recently, Angelucci and De Giorgi (2006), using the same data set used in Hoddinott, Skoufias, and Washburn (2000), corroborated that result. They found that between 1998 and 1999 only five of thirty-six food items experienced a price increase in program localities; moreover, among the food items whose price did not increase were rice, beans, maize, and chicken.[13]

Saving and Investment

There are at least three channels through which Progresa-Oportunidades can affect saving and investment. First, household consumption might not increase by the full amount of the income transfer, augmenting household savings, which can be allocated to investments in financial or physical assets. Second, higher and more predictable consumption derived from program transfers might allow households to invest in riskier projects, with higher expected returns. And third, households' increased wealth might improve their access to credit. There have been few evaluations of the program's impact on investment and none that have attempted to separate these three channels, thereby providing measures of how program households' access to credit or attitudes toward risk change.

Gertler, Martinez and Rubio (2005) focused on the impact of Progresa-Oportunidades on rural households that have been in the program 5.5 and 3.5 years and on a set of controls. The authors measured the effects of the program and the effects of differential exposure (reflecting cumulative effects). They estimated the program's impact on saving and on the probability of engaging in a microenterprise, of using land for productive purposes, and of owning production animals (poultry, cattle, sheep, and the like) or draft animals (horses, oxen, and the like). The authors' hypothesis was that "if the transfer [from Progresa-Oportunidades] helps

---

13. Angelucci and De Giorgi (2006, p. 12). Angelucci and De Giorgi's work is interesting in that they find an important positive effect of Progresa-Oportunidades on consumption of nonpoor households in rural communities where the program operates compared with that of nonpoor households in communities where it had not yet entered. They attribute this spillover effect to the impact of the higher program-induced liquidity in the credit markets of the communities where it operates. The issue is not pursued here because for the most part the effect concerns the nonpoor, but it is worth noting not only because of the inherent value of this potential positive externality, but also because it might contradict the assumption that the program has no effect on the nontreatment group. A similar spillover effect has been noticed with regard to the program's impact on educational enrollment.

households overcome liquidity constraints or take on an additional risk for investments that boost income and consumption, it is possible that beneficiary households will obtain a permanent increase in living standards which may be sustained even after the program is removed."[14]

The authors found that, on average, rural households in the program had a marginal propensity to consume (MPC) out of the total transfer accumulated during program exposure of 75 percent. That in turn generated 1.2 centavos of additional consumption per peso saved, for an average annual return on investment of 4.8 percent. As a result, households that had been in the program for more than 5.5 years showed a permanent increase in consumption of approximately 22 percent (compared with an increase of 17 percent in households with 3.5 years in the program). Results also showed that program households were more likely than nonprogram households to own production and draft animals (5 percent and 17 percent more likely, respectively) and that the differences increased with program exposure. Participation in a microenterprise (defined as an activity such as sewing clothes, making food for sale, manufacture of handicrafts, carpentry, construction, and the like) also was affected: treatment households were approximately 33 percent more likely to participate than control households. Differences in participation by women were more pronounced (43 percent more likely to participate than men), and they were not associated with domestic services but with activities that require some initial capital expenditure (like handicrafts).[15]

It is important to note that these results do not hold for all households in the program. Approximately 40 percent of rural Progresa households either have no agricultural assets or own no land; another 40 to 45 percent own three hectares or less; and only 13 to 15 percent own more land than that. When those differences were taken into account, the authors found that households with no agricultural assets had an MPC out of program transfers of 91 percent, in contrast with households with three or more hectares, whose MPC was 67 percent. Further, for households with no agricultural assets the return on investment of cumulative transfers was not significantly different from zero, while it was 5 percent for households with three or more hectares. These results suggest that initial ownership of assets is important if an additional income transfer is to have a positive effect on the return on investment. In some cases, this

14. Gertler, Martinez, and Rubio (2005, p. 3).
15. Gertler, Martinez, and Rubio (2005).

additional income transfer, by breaking liquidity constraints, allowing undertaking of a riskier project, or facilitating access to credit, might be enough, if sustained over some period, to trigger an endogenous process of asset accumulation and income generation, eventually making the income transfer unnecessary. But in other cases initial assets might be insufficient (or nonexistent), keeping families in a poverty trap despite the income transfers or requiring substantially more time for the income transfers to generate a self-sustaining process of income generation.[16]

These results are of the essence for Progresa-Oportunidades, given the conceptualization of the program as a temporary investment in the poor. Its central effects will gradually occur through the accumulation of human capital to help younger generations obtain higher lifetime incomes and break the intergenerational transmission of poverty, but that is not incompatible with positive effects on the current generation of poor adults through increased productive investments that might have earlier returns (say after five or six years) than the much longer-term investments associated with the formation of human capital. The few evaluations performed so far show that that might be the case in at least a subset of rural households; clearly, this is an aspect of the program that deserves substantially more research.

One more observation is useful before turning to the program's impact on human capital. Since 2001, the payment mechanism used in some urban areas has relied on transfers deposited in banking institutions, facilitating access to beneficiary households to financial savings, sometimes for the first time. Evaluations have yet to address the issue of whether reducing transaction costs and providing information on banking services might have an impact on poor households' patterns of saving.[17]

---

16. Carter and Barret (2006) develops an analytical framework to distinguish deep-rooted persistent structural poverty from poverty that naturally passes with time due to economic growth. The authors' key hypothesis is that there might be a threshold level of assets under which families are caught in a poverty trap, thus requiring special policies aside from growth to trigger a process of saving, accumulation, and investment. The results of Gertler, Martinez, and Rubio (2005) can be interpreted as preliminary evidence consistent with their hypothesis.

17. According to the Coordinación Nacional del Programa de Desarollo Humano Oportunidades (Coordinating Agency for the Human Development Program Oportunidades), the government agency that runs Progresa-Oportunidades, in 2005 there were 1.2 million program households with accounts in commercial banks, into which an average deposit of 960 pesos (approximately US$90) was made bimonthly .

Impact Evaluation: Nutrition and Health

This section reviews the impact of the program on various health and nutritional indicators. To facilitate the discussion, the analysis separates the impacts on different age and gender groups.

Use of Health Services by All Household Members

Progresa-Oportunidades has boosted the use of preventive health services by program participants. Gertler (2000) estimated that during the first two years of the program, demand for services in rural areas increased between 30 percent and 50 percent depending on the age group.[18] The increase represented new visits for preventive care by families that had not previously frequented public health care services, inasmuch as there was no observed substitution of those visits for private health care services. Visits to monitor nutritional status increased by 30 to 60 percent for infants up to two years of age and by 25 to 45 percent for children three to five years of age. Hernández and Huerta (2000) observed a 6 percent increase in the number of children from birth to two years of age brought in for growth and weight monitoring. They also noted that among the visiting families the mother's level of schooling and the distance from the health care unit no longer were associated with the likelihood of showing up for nutritional surveillance, thus breaking the circle wherein children who live in remote communities and whose mothers have little schooling tend not to use health care services. Similarly, Huerta and Martínez (2000) found that participation in Progresa resulted in an increase from 8 to 25 percent in the number of children over two years of age who visited a health unit for the first time. Bautista and others (2004) observed a 67 percent difference in demand for health care services between program and nonprogram communities in 2002. Preventive care visits grew fivefold during 1997–2002 and nutrition-related visits grew by 45 percent, coupled with a drop in the number of visits for severely malnourished children.

Progresa-Oportunidades appears to have had an impact on the use of hospital services. For the same set of rural households, Gertler (2000) found a 58 percent drop in hospital visits for the birth-to-age-two group

18. At program start-up, the use of health care services in rural areas was very low, at 0.65 visits per person per year.

and a considerable decrease in the over-fifty age group. That is consistent with the claim that the program helps to reduce the incidence of severe disease by shifting the focus from an approach that focuses essentially on treatment toward one that places greater emphasis on prevention.

Gutierrez and others (2004b) reported that the same results also appear in the medium run in the same rural areas and in the short run in urban areas. The authors compared two treatment groups in rural areas incorporated in 1998 and 2000 with a control group constructed with matching methods for 2003. They found that after six years, rural program families demanded 35 percent more preventive health services on average than nonprogram families, although they did not find any differences in the use of hospital services. They also reported that there was a 20 percent reduction in sick days for program participants zero to five years and sixteen to forty-nine years of age, and they found an 18 percent reduction for individuals aged six to forty-nine in families incorporated since 1998. The same study also looked at one-year effects in urban areas, where they found an increase in the use of preventive services, although of a smaller magnitude: use was 20 percent higher for program than for nonprogram families. Interestingly, they also found a reduction in demand for hospital services, consistent with the short-run results reported for rural areas: there was a 2.5 percent decrease in episodes of hospitalization, and when the episodes occurred they were 35 percent shorter. Sick days also were reduced by about 24 percent among individuals aged six to fifteen, and there was a 50 percent reduction among individuals aged sixteen to forty.

The qualitative evaluation by Escobar and González de la Rocha (2003) noted, however, that increased demand has resulted in saturation of health care units. In some cases, that has led units to certify visits of healthy children and adults without actually performing a checkup or to institute a "first come, first served" system rather than take appointments. Certification of beneficiaries reporting to health care services is a key element that merits special attention. Last, in some communities the supply of services did not expand as quickly as demand, resulting in care of lower quality than desired.

Prenatal Care and Infant Mortality

Skoufias (2000) reported an 8 percent increase in the number of first-time prenatal care visits among first-trimester pregnant women. Hernández and Huerta (2000) calculated that beneficiaries who sought prenatal care rose from 84 to 89 percent, an increase of nearly 6 percentage points;

the increase for nonbeneficiaries was 1.5 percentage points. Also worthy of note is the relative increase in care provided by medical and nursing personnel (13 percent and 6 percent, for program and nonprogram families respectively).

Gertler and Fernald (2004) studied the medium-term impact of health and nutrition prenatal interventions on rural children, comparing children in the program since 1998, those incorporated 1.5 years later, and those about to be incorporated in 2003. The first two groups constituted the treatment group (with different exposures), and the third group was the control. Children who were from three to six years of age in 2003 were chosen from the three groups, and from those children, subjects of the same age were tested for cognitive and motor development and social behavior.[19] The authors found in comparing the first two groups with the third that there was an average improvement in eight motor tests of 15 percent for boys and of 10 percent for girls; they also found a 9 percent improvement in a test of social behavior for girls, but no impact for boys. The authors claim that "these results are important and suggest that the effects of the program are of considerable magnitude and significant over the medium run (three to six years). Results not only indicate that children are healthier and have better motor development, but that they are better prepared to enter school and have improved educational achievements."[20] On the other hand, the authors found very low levels of cognitive development in the children and only a small impact of Progresa-Oportunidades on that key dimension, perhaps attributable to the lack of early intellectual stimulation, a component that the program does not incorporate; possible nutritional deficiencies, particularly those related to anemia, may also be a factor, as discussed below.

Barham (2005) measured the impact of Progresa-Oportunidades on rural infant mortality. The author's approach differs from that of most of the evaluations surveyed here, relying on government administrative data instead of the program's household surveys. The author constructed a municipal-level data set on infant mortality for the period 1992–2001 and exploited the gradual phase-in of the program in different municipalities in a model incorporating time fixed effects and changes in the

19. Short- and long-run memory was tracked with Woodcock-Johnson tests; language development with Peabody Vocabulary by Images tests; motor development with MacArthur tests; and social behavior with Achenbach Children's Behavior List.

20. Gertler and Fernald (2004, p. 54); author's translation.

supply of health services. On that basis, she found an average 11 percent decrease in infant mortality rates as a result of the program, with stronger effects in municipalities where Spanish was the first language and where there was access to piped water. No measurements are yet available of the program's impact on urban infant mortality.

Children's Health and Nutritional Status

Gertler (2000) observed that young children in Progresa-Oportunidades communities in rural areas became more resistant to disease as a result of better caloric intake and preventive medical care. Specifically, the incidence of disease among children aged zero to two years dropped 12 percent compared with the incidence among nonprogram children; that figure was 11 percent for children aged three to five. Subsequently, Bautista and others (2004) corroborated that result. The morbidity rate for children born to program households in rural areas was 25 percent lower in the first six months of life than for children in nonprogram households, and a reduction of 39 percent was seen for children aged zero to thirty-six months in the base survey after twenty-four months in the program. The program's impact appears to increase over time, suggesting that benefits may be cumulative.

Behrman and Hoddinott (2000) pointed to a significant impact on growth and the probability of stunting among rural children aged twelve to thirty-six months.[21] The authors also found an increase in height per year of nearly one centimeter more than for nonprogram children; that represents one-sixth of their annual average growth and roughly one-third of the standard deviation for growth. Using the weight-for-age indicator, Huerta and Martinez (2000) observed a 17 percent reduction between 1998 and 1999 in the number of rural children aged five to twenty-three months with moderate to severe malnutrition and a 12 percent decrease in the prevalence of high-risk malnutrition among children aged twenty-four to fifty-nine months.[22] Using the height-for-age indicator, they observed that the prevalence of mild, moderate, and severe malnutrition among children five to twenty-three months of age dropped from 70 to 68 percent. These findings were corroborated by Cabral and

21. The authors mention that stunting of physical growth is the main effect of malnutrition found among rural children. This indicator of chronic malnutrition reflects insufficient food intake from an early age.

22. The authors point out that this indicator is the one most often used to assess the impact of nutrition programs, since weight is sensitive to dietary changes in the short term.

others (2002), which pointed to an increase in the number of children visiting health centers for weight and height monitoring and in the frequency of visits. Before Progresa-Oportunidades, only 8 percent of children over the age of two reported for first-time health visits; after nearly two years of Oportunidades, an increase was noted in both program and nonprogram children (26 and 18 percent, respectively). On the basis of the weight-for-age and height-for-age indicators, the program was observed to have a significant impact in reducing the prevalence of child malnutrition, especially severe malnutrition. The weight-for-age indicator showed a 17 percent drop in the prevalence of moderate and severe malnutrition among rural children aged five to twenty-three months and a 14 percent drop in the number of children with varying degrees of low weight for their age.

A study by the National Institute of Public Health (Instituto Nacional de Salud Pública, 2001) used a sample of a cross-section of rural program families and a control group, gathering information on anthropometric measurements, dietary intake, blood samples, sociodemographic and economic data on families, and acceptance and consumption of nutritional supplements. The study revealed that after one year of program participation, families had better levels of vitamin A and folic acid, owing to better intake of micronutrients from nutritional supplements. The differences in the averages between program and nonprogram populations represented one-half of a standard deviation for vitamin A and one-third of a standard deviation for folic acid. With regard to hemoglobin concentration, the prevalence of anemia was lower (14 percent) and there was a difference in height gain vis-à-vis the control group.[23] There were no significant differences in the percentage of transferin saturation (an indicator of iron status) or in the indicator of zinc status. The study felt that the observed impact on hemoglobin and growth were biologically significant and important from a public health standpoint, especially given the program's short period of operation and the fact that only 42 percent of children in the evaluated communities consumed the supplement regularly for six months or longer.[24] The study recommended evaluating the type of

23. The difference in height was limited to children from families with poor housing conditions and those who consumed the supplement regularly for at least six months.

24. Anemia is an abnormally low concentration of hemoglobin in the blood, which leads to inadequate oxygen supply to cells and tissues. This affects key physical functions, such as physical performance, and many mental functions, such as the ability to pay attention. The main cause of anemia is iron deficiency; see INSP (2001).

fortifiers used in the supplements to ensure the use of iron with higher bioavailability.

The impact of Progresa-Oportunidades on the nutritional status of urban children is reported in Neufeld and others (2004b). This study followed 300 children aged six to twenty-three months in twenty-two urban localities in ten states (thirteen localities with treatment and nine without) from mid-2003 to mid-2004. The authors found a modest improvement in the concentration of hemoglobin in the blood and a mild reduction in the prevalence of anemia in program children, as well as a slight improvement in language acquisition for program boys, though not for girls. Nonetheless, they still found that almost a quarter of all children in treatment localities were anemic, representing a significant public health problem.

Neufeld and others (2004a) studied rural children who had been in the program for more than six years, finding an important positive effect on height for age among boys and girls, a very small effect on hemoglobin concentration, and no impact on anemia.[25] Both studies pointed out, as had INSP (2001) before them, that the persistence of anemia might be due in part to the low absorption of iron in the nutritional supplement.

Yet another finding relevant to children's nutrition is that the nutritional supplements did not lead to a decrease in breast-feeding among rural women; in fact, among children under six months of age it increased slightly, as indicated by Hernández and Huerta (2000). This aspect has not yet been evaluated in the case of urban children.

Though the impacts of Progresa-Oportunidades on child nutrition have been positive, evaluations identify two serious problems. First, the low impact on anemia, found in the evaluations conducted so far for rural children in the short and medium term and for urban children in the short term. This problem is partly associated with the original formula for the nutritional supplement, as the form of iron used could not be properly absorbed by children. Evaluations detected this problem in 2001, although it was not corrected until 2005; currently the nutritional supplement contains iron as iron gluconate instead of iron fumarate, improving its absorption. As part of the change, the supplement's content of folic acid and vitamin C were increased, to prevent congenital malformations of the neural tube and acute respiratory diseases, respectively.

25. The incidence of low height for age, defined as two or more standard deviations less than the median of the reference population, was 12.4 percent less in localities that had been in the program for six years than in those that were not yet incorporated.

The second problem is persistent deficiencies in the regular distribution and proper consumption of nutritional supplements. Behrman and Hoddinott (2000), in the initial evaluation in rural areas, found that less than 60 percent of the children reported receiving them. Neufeld and others (2004c) found that in urban areas only 50 percent of children six to twenty-three months of age consumed the nutritional supplement at least one time a week, the main reason being that the rest did not receive it; furthermore, they found that those that did receive it consumed only about half of the recommended dosage and that consumption declined as indicators of poverty increased (lack of cement floor, carton rooftops, and so forth). Finally, they found a similar situation with regard to consumption of nutritional supplements by pregnant and nursing women. Operational evaluations have produced a similar finding. It must be said, further, that the problem has not been lack of budgetary resources, but deficient supervision and insufficient emphasis on this issue in the talks given at health clinics, which have unnecessarily limited a key program objective. One can only hope that the new iron formula and a renovated supervision effort can remedy the situation, despite the recognition that potential benefits for many poor children may have been permanently forgone.

Adolescent Health

No specific studies have been performed on the impact of Progresa-Oportunidades on health indicators for adolescents. Nevertheless, Gutierrez and others (2004a) studied the effects of the program on this age group with regard to smoking, drinking, and risks associated with sexual activity. The study focuses on both rural and urban areas, using differences in incorporation dates to identify the effects of 5.5 and 4.0 years of program exposure in rural areas and one year of exposure in urban areas. Rural youth who had been in the program for four years or more exhibited a 14 percent reduction in smoking and a 12 percent reduction in drinking in comparison with nonprogram youth (no differences were found between 5.5 and 4.0 years of exposure). In urban areas the reductions were considerably lower, 4 percent and 2 percent respectively, a result that may be attributable either to differences in program exposure or to the more risk-prone urban environment. The study found, however, no impact of the program on risks associated with sexual activity (for example, no change in the use of condoms or in sexually transmitted diseases). In interpreting these results, it is useful to recall that topics specifically related to this age group were not added to the health talks until 2001 (see table 2-4 in chapter 2). Perhaps stronger results can be expected further on.

Adult Health

Progresa-Oportunidades appears to have had an important effect on maternal mortality. Hernández and others (2003) used independent mortality data from the Ministry of Health and the National Statistical Institute for the period 1995–2002. (Their approach is similar to that of Barham [2005] for measuring infant mortality, described previously.) These data were then matched with data for rural localities that did and did not participate in the program. The authors found an 11 percent decrease in maternal mortality in the former group compared with the latter; they also found a 2 percent decrease in infant mortality.

More broadly, the program has had a positive effect on simple health indicators for adults. Gertler (2000) found a 19 percent reduction in the number of days that health-related causes kept rural program beneficiaries aged eighteen to fifty from performing their activities in a normal fashion and an increase of 7.5 percent in their ability to walk without getting tired. A similar impact was observed in adults over fifty years of age, with an additional reduction of 17 percent in the number of days of disability and of 22 percent in the number of days in bed. These outcomes are noteworthy since 36 percent of program beneficiaries are between twenty and forty-nine years of age and 12 percent are over fifty.

Impacts on more complex diseases are lower, however. As in many other countries, Mexico's epidemiological transition implies that chronic diseases like diabetes and hypertension are becoming increasingly prevalent among the population, including the poor. The program's health interventions may contribute to earlier detection as a result of the periodic visits that adults must make to health clinics. Fernald, Gertler, and Olaiz (2004) studied the medium-term impact of the program on rural adults aged twenty to forty-nine years who had been in the program between three and six years and compared them with a similar rural control group constructed with matching methods. They found that for both groups obesity (defined as a body mass index greater than 30) was a serious concern: 20 percent of adults in the treatment group were obese, as were 24 percent of the control group. Program effects were positive but small, showing a reduction in the prevalence of obesity of 6.4 percent. Hypertension (defined as diastolic blood pressure greater than 90 mm/Hg) also was a serious concern for both groups: 37 percent of all adults in the treatment group and 39 percent in the control group were hypertensive. Again, program effects were positive but small, showing a reduction of 7.2 percent. More worrisome is the prevalence of uncontrolled diabetes (defined as glucose greater than 126 mg/dl before the first meal of the day): there was no program impact on this indicator, with 19 percent of all adults in both groups experiencing the condition.

Reproductive Health

Skoufias (2000) found that the program had had a strong, positive impact on contraceptive use in rural households, where program women were more likely to use birth control than nonprogram women.[26] This phenomenon was also observed in Hernández and Huerta (2000), which pointed out that the greatest increase occurred in younger women (ages twenty to twenty-four).

Along with increased use of contraceptives, there was a decrease from 49 percent to 45 percent in the number of program women of child-bearing age who were in stable long-term relationships and had never practiced birth control; for nonprogram women the figure dropped from 48 to 47 percent over the first two years of the program. At the same time, however, there was considerable unmet demand for methods of birth control among rural poor women aged twenty to forty-nine: 42 percent of program women and 44 percent of non-program women did not have access to means of contraception (for the rural population as a whole, it was just under 30 percent). The findings of this study indicate also that the likelihood of contraceptive use increases with the level of schooling, thus confirming the strategy of joint delivery of health and education interventions.

With regard to preventive care for women, the qualitative evaluations by Escobar and González de la Rocha (2000, 2003) reported major advances in acceptance of screening for cancer of the cervix, despite considerable initial resistance by women and their husbands in rural areas. Male physicians were one of the main obstacles cited, since there was a notable difference in acceptance in cases in which screening was done by female physicians or trained nurses. Even so, many of the women interviewed stated that they had not previously had a Pap test done, out of

26. Bautista and others (2004) observed an increase in family planning visits at clinics that serve program beneficiaries as well as at other clinics, without encountering any statistically significant differences between them.

embarrassment or fear.[27] This coincides with a later study, Duarte and others (2004), which found that in rural areas the use of Pap tests was 61 percent lower in nonprogram women than program women.

A later study by Hernández and others (2004) evaluated the impact of Progresa-Oportunidades on the use of family planning methods and medical attention during pregnancy, focusing on women aged fifteen to forty-nine in both rural and urban areas. The study evaluated two- and five-year program impacts in rural areas, comparing households incorporated in 1998, 2000, and 2003; in the 2003 group, control localities were constructed by using matching methods. In urban areas a quasi-experimental method was used in which information was collected on eligible households incorporated in 2002 and compared with information on households to be incorporated in 2004.

In rural areas the authors found no difference in the use of family planning methods between program women incorporated in 1998 and 2000. They did, however, find that 17 percent more of the women had knowledge of family planning methods than women in the control group. They also observed that prenatal medical care for women in the program was closer to the Mexican official norm for pregnancy, birth, and breastfeeding than it was for nonprogram women, although not all interventions were performed in all cases (screening for breast cancer and syphilis, for instance). In urban areas they found a 6 percent increase in women who were knowledgeable about birth control methods; they did not, however, observe any improvements in medical care during pregnancy.

Impact Evaluation: Education and Labor Participation

This section reports the impact of the program on educational indicators. The discussion first centers on the impact on enrollment by grade level and then on other schooling indicators. Results of the impact on the use of time and labor participation by program beneficiaries are presented as well.

School Enrollment

The impact of Progresa-Oportunidades on primary school enrollment has been fairly small. Schultz (2000a) estimated it to be between 0.74 and 1.07 percentage points for boys and between 0.96 and 1.45 percentage

27. Escobar and González de la Rocha (2000).

points for girls in rural areas, where one would expect higher impacts. Subsequently, Parker (2003) indicated that the program had no overall impact on primary enrollment but that it had positive effects on failure and dropout rates. That was ascribed in great part to the fact that Mexico has primary education enrollment rates of more than 90 percent, including those in underprivileged rural areas. Todd and others (2005) found a similar result in urban areas after one year of program operation.[28] As noted below, the program's impact at this level of schooling is mainly on continuation rates and performance.

For secondary school enrollment, Schultz (2000a) observed average increases in enrollment of 11 percent for girls and 7.5 percent for boys in rural areas after two years of program exposure. In particular, for the first year of secondary school (a critical transition year), enrollment levels for program beneficiaries rose 9.4 percentage points. Schultz felt that those increases in schooling would translate into a 6 percent increase in income over the lives of women and a 3 percent increase for men. Hernández, Orozco, and Sotres (2000) found that the greatest impact was observed in beneficiaries whose mothers had lower levels of schooling. In schools where students' mothers averaged three years of schooling, the increase in enrollment was 75 percent higher than in schools where they averaged nine years. That may mean that the effects are stronger when the lag is greater, since children of parents with less schooling tend to drop out of school at younger ages. Comparing pre-program enrollment levels in 1996–97 with those in 2002–03, Parker (2005) found a 24 percent average increase in rural areas (the increase was higher for girls than for boys: 28.7 percent and 15.7 percent, respectively); in urban areas, where the program had just two years of coverage when the measurement was done, the author found a 4 percent increase in enrollment (using data from the 2001–02 school year). Todd and others (2005) also found lower effects in urban areas than in rural ones, but effects were positive in both.[29]

---

28. Todd and others (2005), which illustrates how research techniques have adapted to program evolution, is important from a methodological point of view. As discussed, targeting methods in some urban areas changed around 2001–02 to a preliminary self-selection mechanism. This matters because being or not being in the program is no longer a random process, and the decision to be in the program needs to be modeled as part of the evaluation; the Todd and others study does that.

29. It is too early to measure the impact of finishing secondary school on labor market outcomes for program youth, although it may be significant. A recent World Bank survey on poverty and productivity in Latin America found that "firms overwhelmingly choose to

In light of these results and of the higher rates of return for students who finish high school, Skoufias (2000) suggested extending education grants to this level and linking them to academic performance. That suggestion led program officials to add three additional years of education grants as of 2001, although they were not linked to performance.

The impact of additional scholarships on high school enrollment was studied by Parker, who found that results at that level "can only be considered overwhelmingly positive."[30] Comparing the 2002–03 and the 2000–01 school years, she found an increase in enrollment in the first year of high school of almost 85 percent in rural areas and of 10 percent in urban areas. Parker's quantitative measurements coincide with the qualitative assessments of Escobar and González de la Rocha, who in 2004 analyzed four rural communities that they had previously evaluated in 1999 and 2000. The authors found that "if the most important effect on schooling in our evaluations of previous years was in primary and secondary levels, this time it doubtless is at the high school level."[31]

Effects of Differences in Incorporation Period and Program Exposure

Since Progresa-Oportunidades has been in place longer in some areas than in others, it is possible to measure the different effects of having spent more or less time in the program and to follow the impact of the program over the life cycle of children and young people. Two sets of results are available, in Behrman, Parker and Todd (2004) and Parker, Behrman, and Todd (2005). Both studies measure the impact of earlier

---

train skilled (secondary education or above) workers. This is an exceptionally robust finding that is salient in cross-country household surveys, administrative databases, and firm panel data sets. Although the likelihood of training increases with all levels of education, the critical threshold seems to be completion of secondary education. This most likely reflects the idea that investment in training requires a sufficient prior skill base in order to pay off" (Arias and others, 2005, p. 19).

30. Parker (2005, p. 19); author's translation.

31. Escobar and González de la Rocha (2004, p. 251); author's translation. The authors also note a spillover or demonstration effect in nonprogram households, which also sent their young people to school more often. An interesting observation made by the authors is that this might bias (presumably downward) the impacts obtained in quantitative comparisons of treatment and control groups, as control groups also are indirectly affected by the program. More technically, this might violate the assumption that there is no program impact on the control group; see Skoufias (2005, chapter 3) for a discussion.

and later program treatment using double difference methods to compare rural households incorporated in 1997 and in 1999 (with 5.5 and four years in the program, respectively, at the time of measurement in 2003). In addition, both studies used matching methods to compare households with 5.5 years in the program with households that had been selected to enter in 2003 but had not yet received benefits.

The first study analyzes the evolution of three sets of infants and children who in 1997 were between zero and two years of age, three and five years of age, and six and eight years of age. Infants zero to two years old who entered the program in 1997 benefited directly from the program's health component and nutritional supplements but initially not from school scholarships; children three to five years old benefited from the health component (and later from the school scholarships) but not from the nutritional supplements; and children six to eight years old benefited from the beginning from the school scholarships and the health component but not from the nutritional supplements (although all of them might have benefited indirectly from the higher incomes prevailing in the household). For the first group, matching evidence shows that when infants in the program eventually start their educational life, they have a greater probability of advancing consecutively through each school year and of finishing more school years than nonprogram children. These are, of course, initial results, as these children were just beginning their careers, but they may be indicative of positive feedback from improved nutrition and better health to higher school attainment. For the second group the results were weaker, although boys showed a lower probability of failing in a given year (results for girls were not significant). For the third group the effects were unquestionably positive: boys in the program had between 0.42 and 0.90 of a year of additional schooling compared with boys outside the program, and girls had 0.73 of an additional year; both also showed better progression rates and better enrollment rates in secondary school (none of them had yet reached high school).

The second study found that in rural households a 1.5-year difference in program exposure translated into 2.5 percent additional years of schooling (or a 0.2 higher grade level). Comparing youngsters nine to twelve years of age in 1997 who had been in the program since then with youngsters who were about to enter the program in 2003, they found a 14 percent difference in years of schooling (approximately one grade level more). Interestingly, they found slightly stronger effects for boys than for girls (a 1.14 higher grade level compared with a 0.94 higher grade level, respectively).[32]

The Parker, Behrman, and Todd (2005) results, on the whole, corroborate previous findings on the effects of Progresa-Oportunidades on enrollment, but they also raise further issues: first, program effects appeared to be cumulative; second, it mattered when and at what age household members entered the program; third, better nutrition and health seemed to improve school performance. One could presume, on the basis of their results, that infants who had been in the program since birth (or, in fact, infants born to mothers who benefited from the program while pregnant) would benefit the most over the course of their lifetime. On the other hand, their results also indicate that the last set of urban infants incorporated in 2003–04 may need the program until approximately 2023! The point here, developed further in chapter 4, is the need for long-run program continuity, given the program's life-cycle approach.

Educational Attainment

The Ministry of Public Education administered standardized achievement tests to students in the evaluation sample at some 500 primary and secondary schools to which Progresa-Oportunidades families had access. Two tests were used: an assessment of primary education and a national standardized test. Both included sections on mathematics and Spanish. No significant program impact on academic performance was observed. That may be ascribed in part to the fact that jumps in enrollment exert pressure on school resources; reduced resources, in turn, may cancel out students' cognitive achievement gains, as suggested in Behrman, Sengupta, and Todd (2000). That possibility is corroborated in Escobar and González de la Rocha (2000), which notes that all teachers reported higher attendance; however, teachers were almost unanimously agreed that performance had not improved as much as attendance.

More recently, Parker, Behrman, and Todd (2005) found that in rural areas children who had been in the program for five years or more advanced more rapidly through school. The proportion of boys who advanced regularly through school (meaning that they completed at least

---

32. For example, if students not in the program went to school for six years, students in the program went for 6.15 years (6 x 1.025). By being in school 0.15 more years, they achieved a 0.2 higher grade level (conceptually assuming that grade levels—third, fourth, fifth, and so on—can be broken into units).

five years of school in a six-year period) was 64 percent for those in the program and 38 percent for those not in the program; for girls the percentages were 39 percent and 30 percent, respectively. The authors also found some positive, although less conclusive, results on achievement: boys who were ten years old in 1997 (sixteen years old in 2003) had 7 percent better grades in mathematics, 8.1 percent better grades in reading, and 10.4 better grades in writing; for girls significant effects were found only in writing (7.6 percent higher).[33] Parallel work in Todd and others (2005) for urban areas showed that after one year, participation in the program increased significantly (between 10 and 20 percent) the share of boys aged six to eighteen and girls aged six to fourteen who accumulated one more year of school; the study also found that the program increased the amount of time devoted to study by about one hour a week.

Dropout, Failure, and Repeat Rates

Behrman, Sengupta, and Todd (2001) found that after rural households had been in the program two years, children in the households entered school at younger ages; their passing rates were higher, as were reenrollment rates; and repetition and dropout rates were lower, especially during the transition from primary to secondary school. Special mention was made of the impact on grade-to-grade progression observed for children not yet receiving program grants, which suggests a forward-looking attitude on the part of parents. A comparison between boys and girls showed that, in the absence of any intervention, girls tended to progress more rapidly than boys during primary school; however, girls were more likely to drop out of secondary school and not return. Accordingly, the authors felt that longer participation in the program for children aged six to fourteen would increase the average level of schooling by an estimated additional 0.6 years and increase the number of boys and girls attending secondary school by 19 percent.[34]

Parker (2003) presented preliminary data indicating that Progresa-Oportunidades had reduced dropout and failure rates (especially for

33. The baseline data set did not include measurements on achievement, so matching methods had to be used. Achievement indicators were results on the Woodstock-Johnson tests.

34. For children aged six to ten, participation in the program was associated with lower repeat rates and better progression; for the eleven- to fourteen-year-olds, the associated impact was lower dropout rates, especially during the transition from primary to secondary education, and better reenrollment rates among those who had dropped out of school before entering the program.

girls), mainly in the third and fourth years of primary education in rural areas. In 2000, around 14 percent of boys and 18 percent of girls who had dropped out of third grade were now staying in school as a result of the program; a similar observation was made for the roughly 16 percent of girls who had dropped out of the fourth grade. With regard to failure rates, more than 3.8 percent of boys and 8.4 percent of girls who had failed third grade (and 6.5 percent of girls who had failed grade four) were now passing with the program. Parker concluded that the program seemed to have had an important impact on dropout and failure rates at the primary level, at least in rural areas. Behrman, Sengupta, and Todd (2001) found a significant impact in terms of lowering repeat rates in rural areas, supporting the view that the program's impact at the primary level was on continuation rates and performance, not on attendance. Todd and others (2005) found an almost 24 percent decrease in the dropout rate for children in urban areas after only one year in the program.

Labor Participation

Parker and Skoufias (2000, 2001) showed significant increases in school attendance by boys and girls, coupled with a considerable reduction in their labor market participation. The reduction tended to be less than the gains in school attendance, especially for girls, which suggests that girls combine school work with work at home. For boys, the largest reduction in labor participation—roughly 40 percent from the pre-program level—was among twelve- to thirteen-year-olds. Progresa-Oportunidades did not appear to have negatively influenced work incentives among adult men and women, since no impact was found on their participation in the labor market, either for wage-earning or other types of work (for example, self-employment and unpaid work).

More recent measurements in rural areas in Parker, Behrman, and Todd (2005) showed that children who had been in the program since the beginning (5.5 years at the time of measurement) experienced a substantial reduction in the probability of working. For boys ten and fourteen years of age in 1997 (sixteen and twenty in 2003), the probability was 35 and 29 percent lower, respectively, than for nonprogram boys; the authors also found negative and significant effects with regard to the probability of engaging in agricultural labor. Todd and others (2005) found that in urban areas, after just one year in the program, there was a reduction of 24 percent in male youth aged nineteen to twenty who worked and of 5 percent in females aged fifteen to eighteen.

The qualitative evaluation in Escobar and González de la Rocha (2000) noted a significant program impact on absenteeism in rural areas, with teachers reporting that children who used to skip school to engage in fishing, harvesting, or construction work were no longer missing classes. The evaluation also found that men usually did not stop working when women received the monetary benefits under the program, nor did they send less money home when they worked outside the community.

Impact Evaluation: Targeting Techniques and Poverty Indexes

This section discusses the results of studies that evaluate the accuracy of the techniques used to identify program beneficiaries. It also describes the effects of the program on poverty, using different poverty indexes.

Targeting Techniques

The methods used in Progresa-Oportunidades for selecting beneficiaries are sound, although they lose some of their power of differentiation in relatively richer communities and with households that are very close to the poverty line. Behrman, Davis, and Skoufias (1999) showed that loss of discrimination in the context of rural targeting. Their evaluation indicated that the household targeting method used by Progresa-Oportunidades was the most cost effective for reducing the depth and severity of poverty in comparison with consumption-based targeting or geographic targeting at the community rather than household level. The authors also argued that the discriminant analysis used in the point system for targeting beneficiaries led to some exclusion errors, particularly against small households or households without small children. Those findings led program administrators to make adjustments to the point system in successive rounds of coverage expansion.

As already mentioned, as the program entered larger urban areas it was no longer feasible to visit and gather data for all households in the locality. Hence a mixed method was used. In urban agglomerations classified as having high or very high marginality indexes, complete household surveys were realized, as in rural areas.[35] In other urban agglomerations, a preliminary self-selection of families into the program was

35. These urban agglomerations are called "áreas geoestadiísticas básicas" (AGEBs) (basic geostatistical areas) by the Instituto Nacional de Estadística, Geografía, e Informática (National Institute of Statistics, Geography, and Information Technology).

introduced, consisting of two parts: first, families could voluntarily come to a program module and request incorporation. Second, at that point, household information would be collected (first at the module and then at the household), the point system applied, and an enrollment decision made. Two assessments of this method are available: a quantitative analysis, Coady and Parker (2004), and a qualitative evaluation, Escobar and González de la Rocha (2003).

Coady and Parker (2004) evaluated the urban coverage of Progresa-Oportunidades in 2002, at a time when the program was still incorporating families (urban incorporation continued until 2004). Assuming full coverage, they estimated an exclusion error of almost 24 percent—that is, of all poor urban households, 24 percent were not in the program. They also found an inclusion error of 22.2 percent—that is, of all urban households covered, 22.2 percent were not poor. However, 70 percent of the erroneously included households (15.6 percent of the total number of households) were close to the poverty line, so the inclusion error does not appear to be very important.

Although the results showed that there was room for improvement, they were nonetheless very good by international standards.[36] The main problem seemed to be one of access to information, as the authors found that of all urban poor households that knew about the program, 92 percent requested incorporation (and of those, 80 percent were accepted and 20 percent were wrongly rejected). It is important to repeat this evaluation, since knowledge about the program in urban areas must have increased with the incorporations done in 2003 and 2004.

On the other hand, Escobar and González de la Rocha (2003) found that the "module" selection method was better than carrying out only household surveys, because before surveyors might have missed some poor households in urban areas; thus exclusion errors were lowered. They also found that individuals valued this option because it bypasses political affiliations and local leaders. They pointed out, however, that

36. Coady and Parker compared their results with data for 122 targeted programs in developing countries. The median indicator for those countries showed that poor households received 25 percent more benefits with targeting than without. For the urban Progresa-Oportunidades program they found that poor households received 62 to 100 percent more and concluded that "Oportunidades's targeting performance in urban areas compares very favorably with that of other social programs in developing countries and in Latin America" (Coady and Parker 2004, p. 198; author's translation).

self-selection might lead to the self-exclusion of households that do not consider themselves to be candidates for Progresa-Oportunidades, although they are indeed poor.[37] Finally, they pointed out that while most individuals in the area did know about the program, some were skeptical, reflecting a general lack of credibility in government programs.

Poverty Indexes

Behrman, Davis, and Skoufias (1999) observed that Progresa-Oportunidades reduced by nearly 16 percent the share of the population in underprivileged rural communities having incomes below the poverty line. Foster-Greer-Thorbecke (FGT) indicators showed that the poverty gap index fell by 42 percent, while the severity of poverty index dropped by 58 percent. Their evaluation therefore suggests that the greatest reductions in poverty were being achieved in the poorest households.[38]

More recently, in Cortes, Solís, and Banegas (2006), the National Household Income-Expenditure Surveys published by the National Institute of Statistics were used to compute FGT poverty indexes for three different poverty lines, taking advantage of the fact that as of 2002 the surveys contained an explicit identification of households receiving program transfers. (Unfortunately, the corresponding surveys for 1998 and 2000 fail to do so.) They compared the head count, poverty gap, and severity of poverty indexes for program households with and without the associated transfers in rural and urban areas (although coverage in urban areas was still expanding at that time). For the poverty line associated with the

37. Issues associated with "tagging" or "reputation" effects could play a role here. They have not been analyzed in the context of Progresa-Oportunidades, although they do not appear to be substantive. Take-up in the program has been very high, and the problem has been mostly the opposite, with households outside of the program wanting to be incorporated.

38. The Foster-Greer-Thorbecke (FGT) measures of poverty generate three individual indexes. The first is the head count ratio, which is simply the number of those living below the poverty line divided by the total population of the country. The second is the poverty gap index, which multiplies the head count ratio by the total amount of resources required to bring the poor up to the poverty line. The third is the severity of poverty index, which sums up the square of the difference between the poverty line and the income of each household below the poverty line. The first index gives the proportion of poor people in the national population; the second measures how many resources are required to ensure that all the poor have an income equal to the poverty line. The third gives more attention to the poverty of the poorest of the poor, since the difference between their income and the poverty line is given more weight than the difference for poor families that are closer to the poverty line.

program's targeting method, they found that in rural areas the head count, poverty gap, and severity indexes for 2004 fell by 9.7, 18.7, and 28.7 percent, respectively, while in urban areas they fell by 2.6, 4.9, and 1.7 percent, respectively. The greatest impact, clearly, was in the poverty gap and severity of poverty indexes, reflecting that Progresa-Oportunidades appropriately targets the poorest of the poor, even though the transfers are by themselves not sufficient to push these households over the poverty line (thus having small effects on the head count ratio).

Impact Evaluation: Income Transfers and Regional Markets

This section summarizes results of studies of the impact of Progresa-Oportunidades transfers on income distribution, ignoring its effects on human capital formation. The discussion centers on use of the program to compensate for exogenous shocks and the program's effects on regional markets.

Income Transfers and Unexpected Shocks

As argued in chapter 1, in countries with high income inequality, direct income transfers are more efficient and effective than consumption subsidies in increasing poor households' income and hence consumption. Ignoring its impacts on human capital formation, Progresa-Oportunidades can be seen as a mechanism to transfer income to the poor, in principle for any purpose. In particular, however, it can be used to protect poor households from the negative effects of unexpected income shocks or large relative price changes. Neither of these two possible uses of the program has been subject to a direct evaluation, as they have not been observed. Nonetheless, two results are worth mentioning. First, Davis, Handa and Soto (2001) used a simulation model to show that if Oportunidades had been in place during the 1995 economic crisis, the rural poverty gap and the square of the rural poverty gap would have been 17 percent and 23 percent lower, respectively, in the year following the crisis. Those results are based on the observed coverage of the program in 2001 and presumably would be larger now.

Second, Dávila and Levy (2003) showed that the program could serve to compensate poor households from the income loss associated with the removal of Mexico's exemptions to the value-added tax (VAT), when the price to consumers of previously exempt goods increased (that is, it could be used to carry out a "Slutsky compensation" so that poor households' utility did not fall). More precisely, they calculated that if the program's food transfers were increased by the exact amount of the negative income effect on poor households produced by the VAT increase, a tax reform that eliminates all VAT exemptions could both increase government revenues net of compensation costs and keep constant poor households' real income (in fact, poor households could be overcompensated, with still substantial net tax revenues left over after the compensations were paid for, making the reform potentially redistributive).

These two results may be important for countries facing short-run macroeconomic shocks or large relative price distortions that need to be corrected. They also highlight the distinction between the "conditional" and the "cash transfer" parts of Progresa-Oportunidades, discussed in the next chapter.

Development of Regional Markets

The replacement of food subsidies and food items with cash income transfers has important implications for food producers in rural areas, some of whom may be beneficiaries of Progresa-Oportunidades. Clearly, from the point of view of a small rural producer with marketable surpluses of maize, beans, or similar products, there is a substantial difference between having more consumers in the community with greater income levels and having food items distributed at no cost or sold at a discount in the community by a government agency. In the first case, the communities' increased purchasing power may translate into higher demand for the producer's goods; in the second, the producer faces possibly unfair competition, as he or she has to compete with another supplier who receives government subsidies. (In terms of standard international trade theory, this could be labeled dumping. The phenomenon has been mentioned in the context of international food aid.)

When Progresa was being designed, that was yet another reason for the proposed change to cash transfers.[39] It was expected that the additional monetary income in small rural communities would be an incentive for local producers, having a "multiplier effect" in the local economy (not only for producers of maize and beans but also for small poultry and sheep farmers and the like, whose lower transport and storage costs

---

39. See Dávila and Levy (1996). This theme is developed further in a simple model of Ricardian rents in Dávila and Levy (2004) and is used to help explain the phenomenon of population dispersion.

might give them a comparative advantage).[40] In communities where public stores operated, that effect would perhaps be strengthened by the relative price adjustment associated with phasing out food subsidies.

So far this aspect of Progresa-Oportunidades has been subject to little research, however. The program's impact on regional markets was examined only in the qualitative evaluation carried out by Mexico's Center for Research and Advanced Studies in Social Anthropology (CIESAS).[41] Inasmuch as women spend most of their money on food and buy their groceries at local stores or from street vendors, the evaluation found a positive impact on the flow of economic resources within regions and communities, reflected in a more buoyant regional economy. Some instances also were observed of women beneficiaries investing in small-scale livestock cooperative projects (Escobar and González de la Rocha, 2000). The results of Gertler, Martinez, and Rubio (2005) are consistent with these observations, although in their case the additional investments came from saving part of the program transfers. In small rural areas, higher spending by program households is a potential additional channel for creating income-earning opportunities for the poor.[42]

Impact Evaluations: Intrahousehold Relations and Women's Status

Mothers play a central role in Progresa-Oportunidades, as recipients of income transfers for the whole household, as the household members

40. There are 70,993 localities of 2,500 inhabitants or less in Progresa-Oportunidades; in 83 percent of them, more than 75 percent of the population benefits from the program. Assuming an average increase in real (monetary) incomes of 20 percent coming from program transfers, these 58,924 localities would experience a 15 percent real increase in their aggregate purchasing power. (This is a lower-bound figure, since program transfers probably represent more than a 20 percent increase in cash income in these localities; they are among the poorest of all, and in some almost all households are in the program.) See table 2-2 in chapter 2.

41. See Oportunidades (2005e) for the evaluation, which was conducted by Escobar and Gonzáles de la Rocha, two researchers with CIESAS.

42. Relative prices for rural consumers, particularly for food, are now on the whole free of distortions. The same is not true, however, for prices paid to producers of agricultural products. This maintains an incentive for population dispersion and eliminates some of the benefits associated with economies of scale and agglomeration in rural localities derived from the increased monetization of transactions. Further, producer subsidies might act as a tax on small rural producers who are net buyers, particularly in the case of maize; see Levy and van Wijnbergen (1992). These interactions, which are relevant for poverty policy in Mexico, need more research.

bearing principal responsibility for complying with program conditions (hopefully with fathers' support), as the contacts for program officials, and as beneficiaries of some of the health interventions. In principle, one might expect changes in the balance of power within the family regarding decisions on spending, school attendance, and family size, among others, when women receive income transfers directly. Nevertheless, few evaluations have attempted to measure such impacts, given the methodological difficulties in doing so and the lack of systematic data. As a study by Adato and others pointed out: "Nevertheless, household surveys are blunt instruments with which to examine intrahousehold relations, because the context of such decisions is often unstated, and without adequate understanding of the sociocultural context, survey results can easily be misinterpreted."[43] Two studies by these authors are available, focused on rural program households during the first two years of enrollment. Using a mix of household surveys and interview techniques, they found a gradual change in bargaining relations, with women increasingly deciding the pattern of spending of the program's transfers. Program women supported the principle of designating women as principal beneficiaries, despite the extra burdens that the program placed on them (for example, from having to travel to receive the transfers and to attend the health talks). They sensed a new empowerment in not having to ask their husbands for money every time that they wanted to buy something; they also reported increased freedom of movement and an "opening up of their minds" because they had more exposure to the world outside their homes and more responsibility. In sum, "the research thus suggests that women are benefiting from a new recognition of their importance in the family, new freedom of movement, and some increased confidence, awareness, and knowledge, without paying a major price in terms of intrahousehold harmony. Nevertheless, the changes in intrahousehold relations brought about by the program appear to be modest. This should not come as a surprise or disappointment, however, as change in this domain is necessarily slow as well as complex where women make strategic choices involving challenge, conformity, and accommodation. Progresa gives women new resources and information with which to approach these choices."[44]

The more recent qualitative evaluations seem to confirm these trends. Escobar and González de la Rocha, in a study of the impact of Progresa-

43. Adato and others (2000, p. vi).
44. Adato and others (2000, p. xv).

Oportunidades on urban households, observed that "delivery of resources to women as well as the health talks and the social pressures that come with it facilitate the application of these resources by women with less interference from other household members. But autonomy in administration does not imply full women's autonomy. Women improve their ability to do what they think is best for the family, not for themselves. But this improvement gives them satisfaction and a sense of well-being. Women are clear in this regard. All focus groups with women manifest the value attached to this improvement."[45] Similar findings are reported in their medium-term evaluation of rural areas, in which they also noted the increasing role of grandmothers in child rearing and household administration in program families, given that mothers worked more and fathers frequently migrate.[46]

Impact Evaluations: Migration

Rubalcava and Teruel (2005) focused on the impact of Progresa-Oportunidades on the demographic composition of households and their migration decisions. Particular attention was given to the concept of "household" since that is the program's basic target unit and to the possibility that its composition might change in response to the program's income transfers as families tried to maximize their value or prolong their duration. The authors also considered how the program's positive income shock affected migration of household members. They followed household dynamics over the period 1997–2003 in rural areas, using matching methods to compare changes in households' demographic composition in treatment and control localities (the latter were localities about to be incorporated in 2003). The longitudinal database constructed allowed them to detect individuals that remained, entered, or left the household because of marriage, death, migration, or other causes.

Rubalcava and Teruel found, on one hand, that program households were slightly larger, as sons and daughters seven to fifteen years of age returned to the family to attend school (it is not uncommon for poor rural families to send their children to live with better-off relatives in the city)

45. Escobar and González de la Rocha (2003, p. 326); author's translation.
46. Escobar and González de la Rocha (2004, p. 249).

or as elderly members reincorporated themselves into the household.[47] On the other hand, they found that female program beneficiaries migrated more than nonbeneficiaries to other communities to start their own households and that male program youth aged thirteen to twenty-one exhibited a higher probability than nonprogram youth of migrating to another state or even abroad, principally to the United States. Most of those effects, however, were quantitatively small, though statistically significant. Further follow-up is required to determine whether those tendencies are more pronounced in program than in nonprogram families and whether there are other effects on family composition.

Angelucci (2005) focused on the impact of Progresa-Oportunidades on migration. The hypothesis, consistent with the overall aims of the program, was that the positive income shock associated with the program might relax households' credit constraints and allow households to finance migration activities or, alternatively, that by reducing the variance in their consumption, the program might permit them to undertake riskier activities, like migrating (particularly abroad). Angelucci's results are derived from the first set of treatment and control families incorporated in rural areas in 1997–99. From this data set the author observed that 95 percent of all migrant trips in these families were undertaken by individuals between fourteen and forty years of age. She then noted that to the extent that the relevant household members must be in their communities to receive a share of the income transfers (those associated with the education component), the program's effect on them would be to reduce migration. However, older members may benefit from the overall income increase for the household without having to be or remain in the community; hence, program conditions might affect household composition by allowing older members to migrate while younger ones are required to stay. International migration in these households was small: only about 1 percent of both treatment and control families in the sample had a member residing in the United States, and only about 3 percent had one international migrant in the previous year. On the other hand, 13 percent had a domestic migrant. Although the program's effects

---

47. This might be a result of initial deficiencies in the targeting system, which inadvertently left out households with no children, many of which were poor households that included only elderly people. That omission was corrected over 2002–04 as coverage expanded.

started from that low base for international migration (which the study reasonably assumed was mostly to the United States), they were large and significant: "program availability is associated with a 60 percent increase in average migration rate."[48] That finding contrasts with the finding for domestic migration, which showed no statistically significant effects of the program.

The findings of Rubalcava and Teruel and of Angelucci are preliminary, and they may not be fully consistent. Further evaluation is needed to determine the magnitude and composition of these migration flows and the mechanisms by which the program affects them. In addition, a distinction needs to be made between temporary (or circular) and permanent migration. Still, both set of findings are relevant because they focus on an important issue that has so far been insufficiently explored and needs further attention. Clearly, poor households optimize the use of their resources (as do non-poor ones), and relaxing of their income constraints triggers changes that spill over into many dimensions. As seen, most program households use their additional income for consumption (mostly, but not only, for food). The available evidence suggests that a minority of these households also use part of their additional income for investments and that an even smaller minority use them to facilitate migration by some household members. This migration, in turn, might be driven by marital or related reasons (as in Rubalcava and Teruel), but in many cases it most likely is driven by the search for better jobs (as in Angelucci). The latter type of migration, in the end, is just a form of investment, particularly for the subset of poor rural households that have no land or that have land of such poor quality that it is not reasonable to invest in it.[49]

Migration responses by treatment households to the program are, almost by definition, welfare-enhancing from their point of view and thus should be seen as a positive effect of Progresa-Oportunidades. A separate question concerns the impact of the phenomenon on national welfare. That issue is beyond the scope of this book, but two remarks are nonetheless relevant. One, the phenomenon is driven, by and large, by the low productivity of workers when they are employed in Mexico compared with their productivity when they are employed abroad, and it is a

48. Angelucci (2005, p. 23).
49. Migrant remittances are the return on this investment.

reflection of systemic underinvestment in Mexico; it clearly is not a short-coming of Progresa-Oportunidades.[50]

The second remark is forward looking: the international migration currently observed in program households is undertaken, according to Angelucci, either by the parents or older siblings of program children and young people who currently receive an education scholarship. But these program children and youth will gradually finish high school and will no longer be tied down to their localities. Will they, healthier and better edu-cated than the current set of migrants, also migrate abroad, perhaps in larger numbers? Or will they be able to find jobs in Mexico? The issue, put differently, highlights what was mentioned in chapter 1: Progresa-Oportunidades will not directly increase growth, nor is it a substitute for other policies required to enhance growth and stimulate the demand for labor in Mexico (particularly in the formal sector of the labor market).

Results from Operational Evaluations

External evaluators as well as the Ministry of the Comptrollership and the agency that runs Progresa-Oportunidades monitor and evaluate the management of program operations by using two systematic data sources. Collection began in 1998 of data for the first source, which con-sists of sixty-four indicators that track, among other things:

—*Health:* children under nutritional surveillance and women receiving prenatal care; medical visits per pregnant woman; children under two and malnourished children under five who receive food supplements

—*Education:* monthly grant recipients; enrollment by grade and gen-der; terminal efficiency (that is, how many students finish primary school, how many finish secondary school, and how many finish high school); passing, transition, and reenrollment rates

—*Benefits:* amount of payments provided; families that fail to collect benefits; program entrants and dropouts.

Collection began in 2000 of data for the second source, which gathers bimonthly data for a panel sample of 1,000 communities across all states. Every two months, one-sixth of the sample is changed, which enables

---

50. Nor is it that these workers are "unemployable." They have the same human capi-tal, regardless of what side of the border they are on; the difference in their productivity results from differences in the complementary set of assets (land, physical capital, business environment, and so on).

cross-monitoring of a large number of communities. Data are collected for four modules: the community, health clinics, schools, and local Progresa offices.

All in all, operational evaluations show that the quality of program coverage and operation has improved.[51] Still, there have been significant variations during the year and across states. Results indicate the need to shore up the program's logistical function to guarantee the supply of medicines and nutritional supplements; timely delivery of evidence of compliance with the program's health and education requirements; and materials for health talks.[52] Insufficient quality of educational and health services, if unattended, can turn into one of the program's greatest problems.[53]

Summing Up the Evaluation Effort

For more than eight years there has been a large, systematic, and sustained effort to evaluate Progresa-Oportunidades. The program is doubtless the most evaluated social program in Mexico and one that also has received, fortunately, substantial international attention. Dozens of evaluation reports and academic research papers have been written, in addition to many technical notes. This chapter seeks to review the main insights and results of that work. Four general observations complement it.

First, from the wealth of research reports for urban and rural areas and for short- and medium-term impacts (one to six years), one can distill seven key points about the program:

—It is more efficient and cost effective than previous food subsidy programs from the perspective of transferring income to the poor: it targets recipients substantially better, it has a more balanced urban-rural distribution, and, for a given budget, it transfers more income to the poor. Through the program, millions of poor households are receiving support from the government for the first time.

---

51. Meneses and others (2003) and Meneses and others (2004).

52. For instance, Baltasar and others (2003) found that in July-August of 2001–02 there was a sharp drop in the percentage of children and women monitored for health purposes, coinciding with the vacation period and the absence of education grants.

53. Escobar and González de la Rocha (2003) point out in their qualitative evaluation of the program in urban areas that "there is parental dissatisfaction with respect to the quality of education and the treatment that their children receive in school. . . . A constant complaint has to do with teachers missing school, and the few hours of education that their children get. . . . Beneficiaries' satisfaction with regards to health services is variable; satisfaction ranges from very high to very low" (p. 298; author's translation).

—It has a positive impact on the human capital of the poor: families are eating more and have better diets, they are using more preventive health services, and children and young people are going to school more often and probably performing better. These effects appear to be stronger for households that have been in the program longer.

—It contributes to reducing the number of poor households and has a stronger effect on reducing the depth and severity of poverty.

—It is more effective among the poorest of the poor and progressively less effective as households approach the poverty line. To the extent that the poorest of the poor live predominantly in rural areas, effects are stronger there than in urban areas.

—It may be triggering permanent changes in the income-earning capabilities of at least a subset of its beneficiaries, and it may be stimulating local producers in remote rural areas.

—It may be encouraging a gradual shift in intrahousehold relationships, reducing gender inequality.

—It provides the government with a way to help protect poor households from unexpected negative economic shocks.

On the basis of these effects, it is possible to state that the change experienced over the last nine years has been positive. Compared with the dispersed set of generalized and targeted food subsidy programs and isolated health, nutrition, and education interventions that were in place up to the mid-1990s, Progresa-Oportunidades is a better alternative. The effort put into this endeavor has been positive, and the change has been for the better. The program has played an important role in making the poor in Mexico better off today than a decade ago.

Second, using relatively few resources, Mexico is having a large positive impact on poverty. This is, paradoxically, a direct reflection of the country's severe income inequality. Progresa-Oportunidades redistributes less than 0.4 percent of GDP to households in the lowest two deciles of the income distribution.[54] But those resources are essential if these households, which prior to the program received around 2 percent of GDP, are to break away from poverty. From the point of view of the poor, it is a substantial redistribution, but from the point of view of the country as a whole, it is not. In return for a small redistribution to help one of every

54. In a review of public expenditures in Mexico for 2002, the World Bank found that Progresa-Oportunidades was the most redistributive program in the federal budget; see World Bank (2004, chapter 4).

four Mexicans, the country is realizing a key investment with a potentially large social pay-off.

Third, impact and operational evaluations have played an important role in the program's overall development, establishing a dynamic feedback loop connecting program design, operations, and evaluation.[55] Evaluation led to substantive corrections to the targeting system, reducing exclusion and inclusion errors as program coverage expanded; evaluation led (belatedly) to modifications in the formula for nutritional supplements, hopefully enhancing their impact on anemia; evaluation led to the extension of school scholarships for three additional years, generating the largest proportional increases in enrollment; and so on. Operational evaluations have been essential to detect and correct errors and to make improvements in the day-to-day running of the program, notwithstanding the important problems that still need to be addressed.

An essential part of the evaluation effort has been continual interaction between program officials and evaluators. The availability of large databases and a policy of open access and transparency have contributed to an ongoing dialogue between policymakers and researchers (national and international, from both academic and policy institutions).[56] Evaluation is a process, and its different components—data collection, sample design, analysis, debate—have enriched and improved Progresa-Oportunidades.

Fourth, results nevertheless have not been unambiguously positive. Impact and operational evaluations also report that there have been and continue to be problems and deficiencies. Although on balance positive results prevail, that should not give the impression that the program's design and operations are perfect. Some mistakes have been significant, some took to long to correct, and some have yet to be fully corrected. In the absence of those mistakes, the program's impact would have been larger by now (as in the case of anemia, discussed previously). There also have been periods of slack and uncertainty, even confusion, and they may still occur in the future, as discussed in the next chapter. It is wrong to claim that the program—and even less the strategy associated with it—has been a complete success.

55. This role is independent of the role that they have played in program continuity, discussed in the next chapter.

56. To date, nearly 80,000 community surveys and more than 8 million household surveys have been completed, according to the Coordinación Nacional del Programa de Desarrollo Humano Oportunidades.

Progresa-Oportunidades has helped to focus, unify, and give consistency to government food programs, but not entirely. Even after the program attained practically complete coverage in the rural areas in 2002–03, the network of public rural stores operated by Diconsa has continued to receive fiscal subsidies, though less than before (see table 4-1 in chapter 4). These subsidies are difficult to justify on poverty alleviation grounds, and they are probably a response to rent-seeking activities of not-so-poor rural producers who see the stores as an easy channel for marketing their surpluses. A similar situation exists with regard to the milk program operated by Liconsa. Rather than being an anti-poverty program, it now is a marketing channel for national milk producers, who see the program as an easy outlet for part of their production.[57]

These programs barely benefited the poor before Progresa-Oportunidades, and they are now at best redundant, if not prejudicial to the poor. Yet they continue to receive public monies under the rubric of poverty alleviation. Progresa-Oportunidades helped to reduce rent-seeking activities of private producers and distributors of food, notably for bread and tortillas, but it did not eliminate them, at least not yet. Whether the government's purchasing of milk or maize for distribution in a network of public stores is the best policy for these industries (and for social welfare) is a different issue, and it does not pertain to poverty alleviation. Nevertheless, these programs are called anti-poverty programs, and while that label may facilitate the approval of funds by Congress, it generates confusion about their objectives.

The discussion of Diconsa and Liconsa serves to highlight a point about the evaluations of Progresa-Oportunidades: they have all centered on the program itself. This evaluation bias is perhaps inevitable, particularly in the quantitative evaluations summarized previously. But Progresa-Oportunidades was conceived as part of a strategy, and in this overall strategy there has been less consistency than in the program. The fact that current econometric techniques are far from being able to evaluate whole strategies (as opposed to programs or elements of a program) should not obscure the fact that a consistent strategy is better for alleviating poverty than a consistent program. Progresa-Oportunidades does not operate in a vacuum, and it needs the support of other programs and policies, all

57. Diconsa stands for "Distribuidora Conasupo," the public sector firm running these stores. Liconsa stands for "Leche Industrializada Conasupo," the public sector firm producing and distributing milk.

working in the same general direction, to be fully successful. Evaluating the poverty reduction strategy is clearly more difficult than evaluating an individual program like Progresa-Oportunidades, and an evaluation of that strategy has yet to be done.

Progresa-Oportunidades also was designed to avoid program proliferation and to focus the attention of all ministries and agencies involved in developing the human capital of the poor on undertaking a single, unified effort. That goal too has been only partly achieved. While certainly there has been more coordination between government ministries than in the past, in the last few years new programs to enhance the human capital of the poor, particularly in health, have been developed. And while clearly more budgetary resources are needed to improve health services for the poor, it is questionable whether adding a new program, with a new bureaucracy and related paraphernalia, is the best way to spend them. It is even more questionable if, as a result of these new programs, incentives are further distorted in the labor market, most likely reducing the probability that workers from program families will find a job in the formal labor market. As elaborated on in the next chapter, agency coordination and program proliferation are substantive problems. Progresa-Oportunidades has helped to reduce them, but as part of an overall assessment it must be pointed out that the program has not solved them. Again, it is easier to achieve consistency in a program than in a strategy.

CHAPTER FOUR

Program
Institutional
Design

Chapter 2 provided data documenting that Progresa-Oportunidades is a very large program. The results summarized in chapter 3 indicate that despite some operational problems, to date the program has been effective in reaching its initial objectives. In August 2006 the program entered its tenth year of operation, having expanded to cover practically the entire population living in extreme poverty over the course of two different federal government administrations (originating from two distinct political parties). This chapter discusses the main institutional features of the program that have facilitated this outcome. Emphasis is placed on the factors contributing to program scale-up and continuity, and some considerations regarding program replication are discussed.

Gradualism and Budgetary Feasibility

Progresa-Oportunidades was to operate instead of, not in addition to, existing food subsidy programs, which were to be phased out as part of the strategy associated with the new program. That approach made implementation substantially more difficult than it otherwise would have been, but there were two powerful reasons behind the decision.

First, as argued in chapter 1, food subsidy programs were only partially reaching the poor. When they did, they did not enhance the capabilities of the poor; they served only as mechanisms to transfer income.

However, adding income transfers from Progresa-Oportunidades to the income transfers associated with the other food subsidy programs, particularly targeted ones, could have raised the risk of welfare dependence.[1] The internal coherence of the overall poverty alleviation strategy required giving careful consideration to ways to avoid setting policy-induced poverty traps or inadvertently generating incentives for beneficiaries to become permanently dependent on government support. Clearly, after a certain level of transfers, additional resources for poverty alleviation could best be used for infrastructure projects, for temporary employment programs, or for some other projects or programs within the overall poverty alleviation strategy.[2]

A second, equally powerful reason derived from fiscal considerations. Given the very tight budgetary conditions prevailing at that time, a new program would have been feasible only if it did not put additional pressures on the federal budget. Although the short-run macroeconomic adjustment program to the 1994–95 financial crisis was pretty much over by the time Progresa began operation in August 1997, the crisis left large budgetary pressures. To avoid a systemic banking crisis, fiscal resources had to be channeled to prop up many private banks and some development banks. Moreover, the recession, along with the high real

1. That is because targeted income transfers (in-kind or in cash) may have a very large marginal income tax associated with them: if you stop being poor because you have earned additional income through your own efforts, the transfer stops; hence, your additional income is "taxed" in the amount of the targeted income transfer or, put differently, your additional effort generates less "net" income for you. If the targeted income transfer is large, the marginal tax can also be large, generating strong disincentives to work: on balance, it may be best to continue to be poor in order to receive government transfers and work less. See Besley and Kanbur (1990) for a discussion of this issue in the context of poverty programs. From this perspective generalized subsidies are better than targeted subsidies, but, as argued earlier in chapter 1, in a context like Mexico's, which is characterized by a very unequal distribution of aggregate income (and consumption), generalized subsidies are very inefficient transfer instruments. Avoiding a high implicit marginal tax rate was an important consideration in making the largest part of benefits under Progresa-Oportunidades temporary, as discussed in chapter 2.

2. The only exception to the "instead of, not in addition to" rule was the school breakfast program, which the government decided to keep. This program, however, was transferred to state governments, taking advantage of a large decentralization effort that was taking place at the time; see Secretaría de Hacienda y Credito Público (2000). The decision followed both technical and political considerations: on one hand, although the evidence was unclear, school breakfasts could enhance the impact of program benefits on educational performance; on the other, by transferring some resources to the state level, the federal government could in principle count on the support of state governors (or at least the absence of opposition) during the initial stages of Progresa-Oportunidades, while maintaining its objective of operating only one "food subsidy" program itself.

interest rates associated with the adjustment program of 1995, made many private highway projects unviable, and some of them, which had implicit public guarantees, also required fiscal support. Further, pay-as-you-go pensions were being replaced with a prefunded scheme as of 1997, requiring large public resources during the more than twenty-year transition period, particularly in the initial years.[3] Last, as 1998 began, a major unexpected turnaround was observed in the world oil market; prices were rapidly falling, with large budgetary implications for Mexico, whose oil proceeds represented around one-third of all government revenues.[4]

Budgetary pressures thus coincided with the government's desire to launch the new nationwide poverty alleviation program. Under such circumstances, adding another program was not a serious policy option; the real choice lay between keeping existing food subsidies or replacing them with Progresa-Oportunidades. The latter approach would ensure the feasibility of the program even in the absence of tax reform to generate additional revenues or of politically costly budget cuts (which would be added to those already carried out during the macroeconomic adjustment program implemented less than two years before and those associated with the unexpected oil shock). Budgetary feasibility was a key consideration, since the aim of the program was to eventually reach the entire population living in extreme poverty in Mexico (almost one in every three people at that time). Clearly, unless the program's planned scale was feasible from a budgetary point of view, it would be just one more in a long list of many small-scale programs implemented in Mexico in the past.

Table 4-1 shows the evolution of Progresa's budget along with that of other food subsidy programs from 1994 (the year before the crisis) to 2005. Note first that although total resources increased by 30 percent in real terms during that period, they dropped between 1997 and 2001 as a result of the relatively faster phaseout of generalized subsidies in urban areas (first for bread and then for tortillas), which was not offset by one-to-one growth of Progresa-Oportunidades (and the school breakfast program). Thus, during the program's first four years, there was negative net pressure on the federal budget.

---

3. For a quantification of these budgetary pressures, see Secretaría de Hacienda y Crédito Público (1998, 1999 and 2000). The pension reform by itself required additional expenditures of approximately 1 percent of GDP annually.

4. As noted in the federal budget decree for each year, the price of oil in the world market dropped from US$16.50 a barrel in December 1997 to $10.20 in September 1998; a rebound started thereafter.

Table 4-1. *Budget for Food Subsidy Programs, 1994–2005*
Millions of 2005 pesos

Program	1994	1995	1996	1997	1998	1999	2000	2001	2002	2003	2004	2005
Generalized subsidies												
Wheat flour–bread subsidy	7,964	4,769	0	0	0	0	0	0	0	0	0	0
Tortilla subsidy	7,912	9,113	13,775	6,087	1,994	0	0	0	0	0	0	0
Diconsa	3,878	4,200	3,208	1,936	1,103	664	518	616	228	376	1,293	561
Subtotal	19,753	18,082	16,983	8,023	3,097	664	518	616	228	376	1,293	561
Percent of total	72	68	63	45	19	4	3	3	1	1	4	2
Targeted subsidies												
Fidelist tortilla subsidy	1,994	2,068	2,553	2,252	2,427	1,923	1,785	1,500	1,138	225	0	0
Liconsa milk subsidy	2,331	3,165	3,178	2,555	1,826	445	0	2	171	221	405	618
Children in Solidarity food packages	687	831	472	585	418	337	294	277	262	254	239	230
INI food packages[a]	181	225	262	281	281	275	278	286	263	259	261	300
DIF[b]	2,293	2,183	3,272	3,243	2,918	3,107	3,205	3,575	3,826	3,843	3,853	3,393
Progresa	0	0	0	876	5,516	9,592	12,190	15,204	21,179	24,503	26,675	30,151
Others	30	96	126	153	137	140	134	153	151	134	115	111
Subtotal	7,516	8,568	9,863	9,945	13,523	15,819	17,886	20,997	26,990	29,439	31,548	34,803
Percent of total	28	32	37	55	81	96	97	97	99	99	96	98
Total minus wheat flour–bread and tortilla subsidies	11,394	12,768	13,071	11,881	14,626	16,483	18,404	21,613	27,218	29,815	32,841	35,364
Total minus wheat flour–bread subsidy	19,306	21,881	26,846	17,968	16,620	16,483	18,404	21,613	27,218	29,815	32,841	35,364
Total	27,269	26,650	26,846	17,968	16,620	16,483	18,404	21,613	27,218	29,815	32,841	35,364

Source: Author's update of Levy and Rodríguez (2004) with data from the Ministry of Finance.
a. INI = Instituto Nacional Indigenista (National Institute for Indigenous People)
b. DIF = Desarrollo Integral de la Familia (Integral Development of the Family).

Note also that because generalized subsidies for bread and tortillas were withdrawn, total resources remained constant over the period 1994–97 and then grew rapidly, owing essentially to program expansion. To the extent that generalized subsidies did not reach the rural poor and channeled limited benefits to the urban poor, as pointed out in chapter 1, it was by and large feasible to partly protect poor households from the effects of the phaseout of the generalized bread and tortilla subsidies by maintaining existing targeted subsidies until they were replaced by Progresa-Oportunidades.[5] Paradoxically, the inefficiency of generalized food subsidies was an advantage during the period of budgetary adjustment, as their removal was partly the de facto equivalent of an increase in consumption taxes for the non-poor and partly an elimination of rents for all the intermediaries along the maize–maize flour–tortilla chain.

As a result of the gradual phase-out and phase-in strategy, in 2005 just two programs—Progresa-Oportunidades at the federal level and the school breakfast program at the state level—accounted for 93.2 percent of resources for food programs (84 percent under Progresa and 9.2 percent under the school breakfast program).[6] Thus, it is possible to conclude that the 1994–2005 period witnessed a gradual shift in resources from generalized to targeted subsidies (the latter increased 363 percent in real terms) while budget funding remained almost constant (figures based on table 4-1). That translated into a redistribution of income in favor of the poor and the virtual elimination of food subsidies to the non-poor.

An additional implication of the transformation was an inversion in the spatial distribution of resources, as illustrated in figure 4-1. Due to Progresa-Oportunidades, 88.6 percent of all subsidies in 2005 were channeled to rural areas, in contrast to 31.4 percent in 1994. That matches more closely the geographical distribution of poverty in Mexico and the observed differences in its depth and severity.[7]

5. For 90 percent of all poor households who received targeted subsidies prior to Progresa-Oportunidades, the nutritional cash transfer under Progresa-Oportunidades was larger than the monetary value of the targeted transfers that it replaced. When the educational cash transfers are accounted for, all poor households received a larger income transfer under the new program than under the previous programs (Levy and Rodriguez 2004).

6. Reference is made to "food programs" for purposes of comparison only, as Progresa-Oportunidades is not a food subsidy program.

7. At the start of Progresa-Oportunidades, almost 60 percent of all poor households lived in rural areas. Furthermore, the Foster-Greer-Thorbecke index for the depth of poverty was 9.9 times higher in rural areas than in urban ones, and the rural index for the severity of poverty was almost thirteen times higher than the urban index (Levy and Rodriguez 2004).

Figure 4-1. *Composition and Distribution of Federal Funding for Food Subsidies, 1994 and 2005*

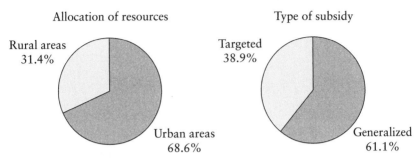

1994
Total $16,963 (millions of 2005 pesos)

Allocation of resources

Type of subsidy

Rural areas
31.4%

Urban areas
68.6%

Targeted
38.9%

Generalized
61.1%

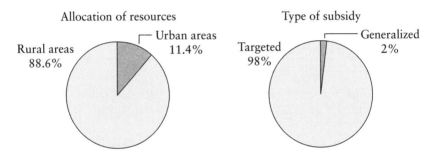

2005
Total $35,364 (millions of 2005 pesos)

Allocation of resources

Type of subsidy

Rural areas
88.6%

Urban areas
11.4%

Targeted
98%

Generalized
2%

Source: Author's update of Levy and Rodriguez (2004) with data from the Ministry of Finance.

To provide a measure of the macroeconomic dimensions of the program, table 4-2 shows the Progresa-Oportunidades budget from 1997 to 2005 as a share of total programmable federal spending and total GDP.[8] In 2005 Progresa-Oportunidades represented an expenditure of 0.36 percent of GDP and 2.29 percent of programmable spending. Its share of GDP has expanded slightly over the last few years, since, as desired, the program has grown much faster than aggregate output. However,

8. Total programmable spending equals total federal spending less interest payments on the public debt and revenue-sharing transfers to states and municipalities.

Table 4-2. *Progresa-Oportunidades Budget as Share of GDP and Programmable Spending, 1997–2005*
Percent

Participants	1997	1998	1999	2000	2001	2002	2003	2004	2005
GDP	0.02	0.09	0.15	0.17	0.22	0.30	0.33	0.34	0.36
Programmable spending	0.09	0.57	0.97	1.12	1.36	1.72	1.81	1.93	2.29

Source: Author's compilation with data from the Ministry of Finance.

because the program has now reached its overall coverage, its share of GDP should gradually fall (assuming positive GDP growth and no additional benefits). That does not mean that resources devoted to poverty alleviation should necessarily fall as a share of GDP in the future; only that further fiscal resources for that purpose could perhaps be more profitably allocated to other components of the poverty strategy, unless, as mentioned, program benefits are increased. All in all, however, it is probably fair to say that Progresa-Oportunidades has not placed an undue burden on the fiscal accounts.

Two more observations on budgetary sustainability are useful. First, it is critical to highlight that the redistribution of income to the poor, particularly the rural poor, associated with the program did not imply either a tax increase or the explicit and brusque elimination of benefits for any group. It actually helped that the strategy for gradually eliminating generalized subsidies, particularly for tortillas, was applied in an inflationary context, because to operate the generalized subsidy, tortillas were subject to a nominal price ceiling determined by administrative fiat.[9] As a result, it was possible, at discrete time intervals, to increase their nominal price faster than the general rate of inflation, until the point at which the price was equal to the no-subsidy equilibrium price. Doing so in an inflationary context was easier than in periods of sustained price stability, when any nominal price increase is more clearly perceived as a real price increase. Further, to the extent that price controls on tortillas were not fully observed across all urban stores, the decreed nominal increases did

9. According to reports published by Banco de México, Mexico's central bank, as a result of the crisis the average inflation rate jumped rapidly from 8.3 percent in 1994 to 37.8 percent in 1995; it then fell gradually to 30.7 percent in 1996, 17.7 percent in 1997, 15.4 percent in 1998, and 15.1 percent in 1999. At that point the generalized tortilla subsidy was fully phased out.

not always imply higher prices for urban consumers; rather, they meant lower rents for all the intermediaries who took advantage of the arbitrage opportunities created by the government-induced distortions along the maize–maize flour–tortilla chain.

The absence of explicit tax increases or large-scale and abrupt reduction of benefits was a critical element in making the program-induced income redistribution politically sustainable. It is an open question whether in the absence of the reallocation of resources described above Progresa-Oportunidades would have been politically feasible or whether it could have attained such a large scope without facing the explicit opposition of some organized group in Congress.

That is not to say that the intermediaries in the tortilla chain passively sat by as the subsidy was eliminated or that some urban groups, particularly in large metropolitan areas, did not protest its elimination and the increases in the price of milk. There were some tense times during which opponents tried to "blackmail" the government by attempting to sabotage the supply of tortillas; by using the media to point out that "a small group of technocrats" in the Finance Ministry was acting against the welfare of the poor;[10] and by organizing protests by groups of beneficiaries of the subsidies, particularly in the case of milk in Mexico City. But those attempts did not have the intended effect. The Finance Ministry received the support of the president to stay the course, the protests were not that large or long-lasting (not that many people had been receiving benefits; moreover, the legitimacy of the organizers of the protests was called into question), and intermediaries in the chain witnessed a determined and consistent strategy on the part of the government to reduce subsidies, including the use of all legal means to ensure an adequate supply of tortillas.

That point is worth noting, because stronger or more sustained political conflicts around the elimination of generalized subsidies, large budgetary reallocations, or tax-financed income redistributions could have been prohibiting constraints in other contexts. In Mexico's case there were substantive political problems, particularly in the initial years when the program had not yet earned credibility, but they were not critical enough to inhibit the initiative altogether. More generally, in contemplating a large-scale program like Progresa-Oportunidades, the issue of how to sustain financing of benefits needs to be addressed as part of program

10. See, for instance, the cover article of the Sunday magazine *Enfoque* of the newspaper *Reforma* for March 24, 1996, under the title "The Hunger Card" (in reference to the proposal to use magnetic cards to pay benefits under Progresa-Oportunidades).

design. Sustainability in this context means identifying non-inflationary sources of funding in the government's budget and achieving a political understanding that can give relative permanence to the funding.

The second observation on sustainability has to do with the pace of change. Fiscal constraints strongly suggested the need for gradual growth of the program's coverage, but aside from those constraints, gradualism also was necessary in order to acquire experience with the program and to correct the many administrative problems that appeared along the way. The sum of budgetary and operational considerations therefore determined the gradual expansion strategy described earlier. Gradualism has helped to ensure the program's sustainability so far, although it implied that eight years of operation were necessary before full coverage was reached. It also allowed for a difficult but still politically manageable approach to phasing out the other food subsidy programs, particularly those that were more sensitive.[11]

A gradual approach, on the other hand, may require more time than allowed by the constitutional mandate of the federal administration that initiates a program. Consequently, in addition to the budgetary considerations above, program design needs to consider what kinds of conditions allow a program to continue growing under an administration that is different from the one that started it.

Availability of Physical Infrastructure

Progresa-Oportunidades was built on the previously existing health and educational infrastructure and, to a large extent, on the administrative

11. Still, it should be noted that in the initial years of the program the federal government received substantial criticism from some members of Congress, journalists, and academics for phasing out generalized food subsidies, particularly for tortillas, even though it was done over the course of four years. In part they derived from an urban-rural imbalance during the program's growth period, when most of the initial resources came from phasing out generalized subsidies in the urban areas and most of the initial growth took place in the more remote rural areas. They also derived from a lack of credibility about the new strategy (or about the government in general) and from the theoretical or ideological belief that social programs should provide universal benefits, not target specific groups as Progresa-Oportunidades did. As positive evaluation results were obtained and as program coverage expanded to larger urban areas, criticisms gradually diminished. Not many voices today call for reestablishing the generalized subsidy for tortillas or reopening Conasupo, the government agency for marketing maize and administering the tortilla subsidy. Nonetheless, the discussion about generalized and targeted subsidies has not been fully settled, and it has recently appeared with regard to nonfood social programs like noncontributory pensions (or minimum pensions).

capacity and personnel already in place.[12] The program's budget did not contemplate having resources for constructing health or educational facilities. Clearly, without the preexisting infrastructure, the program's scope would have been much diminished or its rate of growth restricted to the educational and health sectors' ability to expand their infrastructure pari passu with the program. According to the Coordinación Nacional del Programa de Desarrollo Humano Oportunidades (National Coordinating Agency for the Human Development Program Oportunidades), in 2005 a total of 113,001 schools (80,753 primary schools, 24,617 secondary schools, and 7,631 high schools) and 16,357 health clinics participated in the program. Physical conditions in the clinics and schools vary from locality to locality, and although many of them require maintenance and improvement, they still permit basic operation of the program.

The point here is that it was possible to consider a strategy to subsidize the demand for health and education services only to the extent that a supply of services was previously available, if perhaps not in every single locality and under ideal conditions. Making receipt of program income transfers contingent on poor households' personal actions to enhance their human capital presupposed a positive response from health and education providers. Although not without problems and delays, that response has, by and large, been forthcoming. In its absence, the program would simply have replaced the income transfers implicit in food subsidies with explicit cash transfers. That approach still might have provided some welfare gains given the large preexisting inefficiencies, but they would have been smaller than what appears to have been obtained so far. Moreover, just replacing one system of income transfers with another, without contemplating how they would eventually be phased out, could have created future problems. This may be an important consideration for other cash transfer programs: if they are to be contingent on some behavior, the material conditions for that behavior to actually take place must be reasonably present or they must be created as part of the program.

---

12. As Progresa-Oportunidades expanded, it became clear that service delivery capacity would soon be a constraint on program operation, particularly in the health sector. Thus, with additional resources not counted as part of the program budget, more doctors and nurses were hired. In education more resources were channeled to school maintenance projects. These parallel measures to strengthen the supply of education and health services, while very important for the program's success, were not officially coordinated by program authorities, nor were they formally part of the program; see Levy and Rodriguez (2004) for more details.

Capabilities for Data Gathering and Analysis

Progresa-Oportunidades is a data-intensive project, given its emphasis on targeting extremely poor households in large urban areas and in more than 85,000 small and dispersed rural communities. To that end, the program used existing sources of information, but over time it also has generated a very large database, at least by Mexican standards, of household and locality surveys.

Since the program sought to deliver benefits in the more remote and marginalized rural communities first, it was necessary to identify those communities and verify whether the health and educational services required for program operation were available within a reasonable distance. Data from different ministries and agencies had to be made compatible and statistical techniques applied to design an index of marginality for localities.[13] As the program expanded coverage into increasingly larger urban areas, those techniques were modified to apply to urban settings. Because the program required detailed household information to identify those living in extreme poverty, new questionnaires were constructed, similar to the usual income-expenditure surveys. Over the course of the program more than 8 million household questionnaires have been collected and analyzed.[14] In turn, algorithms were developed to separate poor from non-poor households by means of the point system previously mentioned.

A substantial amount of the work was carried out before Progresa-Oportunidades began, over 1995, 1996, and into mid-1997, along with the conceptual discussions taking place within the federal government. The preparatory work was essential to minimize improvisation and to base as much as possible of the design and operation of the program on recently acquired and verified information. Clearly, none of the work described above could have been possible without the existence of the small but relatively well trained (and motivated) staffs in the different federal ministries and agencies involved in program design. In practice, one important factor in making Progresa-Oportunidades feasible and in allowing it to grow and consolidate over the years has been the ability of

13. Previous work in Mexico had generated marginality indexes for states (thirty-one) and municipalities (almost 2,600). For Progresa-Oportunidades, those indexes were developed for 94,394 localities.

14. There are approximately 26 million households in Mexico.

these personnel to collect and analyze large databases, to design new techniques for targeting and other needs of the program, and to administer it in a reasonably efficient manner.

These remarks seek to highlight an aspect of the program that may not always receive the attention that it deserves: a large-scale and complex program requires, in addition to good technical design, budgetary resources, and physical infrastructure, a cadre of individuals who can perform the necessary analysis and operate the program. Other countries probably have qualified staff similar to or better than Mexico's, but others may not. The point here is that in a program of this nature, the issue of personnel also must be considered as part of program design, along with the trade-offs between program complexity and the practical capability to implement and administer such a large-scale effort.[15]

Interagency Coordination

Coordinating ministries and agencies within the executive branch is problematic in Mexico. Genuine differences in perceptions about the best course of action, bureaucratic inertia, insufficient information about the programs of other ministries, and political infighting for resources, turf, and recognition all combine to give ministries and agencies a "vertical" perspective, focusing attention and resources in their "own" programs.[16]

Progresa-Oportunidades was built on a "horizontal" analysis of programs and projects inside the executive branch with the goal of first identifying and then optimizing the resources devoted by all ministries and agencies to enhancing the human capital of the poor. The integrated approach at the core of the program imposed two administrative requirements: establishment of an entity with sufficient power to effectively coordinate the various participants in the program; and a mechanism for

15. On the other hand, some in Mexico argued at the time that Progresa-Oportunidades was being proposed that it was impossible to operate a program of that nature, particularly in so many remote, dispersed rural communities. What has been shown to be feasible ex post was not so clear ex ante, at least to some. A new program always faces new challenges and may need to overcome some clichéd objections (or entrenched interests hidden behind clichés); the difficulty is finding the right balance between audacity and innovation, on one hand, and overly optimistic assessment of what can be done, on the other. That is very much a case-by-case process.

16. This problem may be present in varying degrees in other countries. In Mexico political considerations contributed to making it particularly acute: until 2000, every president of the country for the last seven decades had previously been a member of the Cabinet.

controlling the program's budget, given that it was distributed across ministries and agencies.[17]

Building on previous experience with multisector programs and with the Campeche pilot program, the program's designers incorporated adjustments to the administrative apparatus of the executive branch. Before the program was launched, it was decided that the "entity with sufficient power to effectively coordinate the various participants in the program" should be a new agency that would be given the legal powers to accomplish the task and whose head would be designated by the president.[18] The Ministry of Finance also received sufficient backing from the president to control the program's budget and to make budget realloca- tions, gradually phase out other food subsidies, and modify administra- tive structures to suit the needs of Progresa-Oportunidades, including, if possible, by closing agencies that were no longer required.

Creating a new unit was easier and faster than attempting to change the functioning and operation of the existing ministries and agencies. Fol- lowing the path of least resistance allowed program designers and admin- istrators to concentrate resources and attention on the fairly complex tasks of program start-up and the initial stages of program scale-up, not on large personnel changes and administrative restructuring, which always are time consuming and politically costly.

But there might be a trade-off between the speed and initial ease of program build-up, on one hand, and the medium-term compatibility of the government's administrative structures with the program's objectives and operational needs on the other. Not all the ministries and agencies involved in Progresa were, so to speak, brought along in the process of change; nor, so far, have all agencies been fully restructured. Nor did they all initially share the new strategy associated with the program or think of themselves as beneficiaries of the process.

17. Resources for program operations and the nutritional cash transfers are budgeted in the Ministry of Social Development; for the health component and the nutritional supple- ment, in the Ministry of Health and the Mexican Institute of Social Security; and for the education component, in the Ministry of Education.

18. From 1997 to mid-2002, the agency was called Coordinación Nacional del Pro- grama de Educación, Salud, y Alimentación (Progresa) and from then on Coordinación Nacional del Programa de Desarrollo Humano Oportunidades. This unit is part of the Min- istry of Social Development, but it has legal operational autonomy. The unit has a technical committee that meets regularly, made up of representatives from the ministries of social development, health, education, and finance and from the Social Security Institute. The technical committee is responsible for strategic decisions; the unit is responsible for instru- mentation and day-to-day operations.

Clearly, the administrative structures previously in place were designed to carry out previous programs; they were not designed to implement a program like Progresa-Oportunidades. And because, in the end, the program was a threat to the existence of the agencies and ministries that ran the previous programs, they most likely would not have done so. The creation of a new unit solved this problem and implicitly postponed the solution of a deeper one. It allowed efficient and rapid program start-up and scale-up, but it bypassed the issue of interministerial ownership of the program. The speed and efficacy gained has not been without a cost: all along, ministry and agency coordination has been—and continues to be—an uphill battle, affecting program sustainability and the overall consistency of the poverty strategy. The program clearly would benefit if incentives were further modified so that the ministries of health and education also considered Progresa-Oportunidades their key program for poverty alleviation, as is the case with the Ministry of Social Development, and contributed to its effective implementation because of their genuine commitment to it and not because of presidential pressure or a legal mandate. (This issue is taken up again in chapter 5.)

On the other hand, the agencies that were in charge of some of the main food subsidy programs replaced by Progresa-Oportunidades but that were not closed do not just sit by idly. In an endless search for resources and, in some sense, space, bureaucracies take on a life of their own. The ability of the program to continue focusing sharply on its objectives would be enhanced if the remaining agencies in charge of the public distribution of food items (urban milk stores and the network of rural stores) were finally closed, as was the case with Conasupo (the agency in charge of the generalized tortilla subsidy). As mentioned, these agencies at present are mostly a marketing facility for agricultural producers; they no longer play any meaningful role in providing income support for the poor. But as long as they remain, the temptation to start a new program—or to expand one that lingers on with no substantive purpose—remains. Completing the administrative restructuring would help to control pressures for program proliferation; it also would eliminate remaining tendencies to enhance the income of the poor through isolated in-kind transfers, without considering their impact in an overall poverty alleviation strategy.

There is another side to this issue: the individuals behind the official titles in the ministries and agencies. For many of these individuals, Progresa-Oportunidades was a drastic change, as budgetary resources drifted away from previous programs and, at the same time, they themselves lost the political attention of many parties: the president, governors, Congress, the media. Some felt a sense of displacement, others an implicit criticism of their previous work.[19] And most of them, if not all, were people who had worked for many years with genuine commitment to alleviating poverty. This side of the issue made the decision to create a new unit for what is now Mexico's largest poverty program more difficult, if perhaps necessary given the prevailing circumstances. Such difficulties may be seen as an inevitable aspect of any profound change. But, with the benefit of hindsight, it seems that perhaps more could have been done by the program's designers and promoters to attenuate the problem, making the change easier for all. Other countries launching similar initiatives may wish to consider this issue.

More generally, Mexico's public sector has not developed appropriate incentives for promoting effective coordination by ministries and agencies. Replacing incentives with presidential pressure has been a temporary solution, not a permanent strategy. Legal considerations aside, effective coordination still depends on the president's will and leadership and on the existence of a few champions within the bureaucracy; it is not a result of well-aligned incentives. Yet long-term program sustainability does depend, eventually, on resolving this issue; presidents change and champions sooner or later fade away. This is a deep-rooted problem that goes beyond Progresa-Oportunidades. The Mexican government has not yet found a mechanism to embed a "horizontal" view of programs in ministries and agencies; the result is not only insufficient coordination, but also program proliferation. Ten years after the program began, incentives still exist for "starting a new initiative," "creating a new program," and "designing a new approach," less as a response to the program's shortcomings than as a quest for political visibility. The absence of a permanent solution represents a contingent risk for the program, and that risk may grow larger when a new federal administration takes over the program in December 2006.

The problem of interministerial coordination is made more difficult at times for reasons other than the dynamics of ministry officials and bureaucratic inertia. Presidents themselves may feel the political need to initiate their own programs, even while previous programs like Progresa-Oportunidades continue. Ministries and agencies, in turn, usually interpret the president's need as a softening of the mandate to collaborate and

---

19. Such feelings are exacerbated at times by media that have a proclivity for magnifying differences between government officials.

coordinate with other ministries on previous programs, as their priorities shift toward implementing the president's "new" program (and toward exploiting ministers' personal possibilities for exposure and advancement). And in a political system like Mexico's, in which members of Congress rotate often given the constitutional prohibition against immediate reelection, the legislative branch is weakly positioned to ensure interministerial collaboration through its oversight functions.

It is difficult to determine the relevance of these issues to other countries. The administrative structures and incentives of agencies and ministries vary widely across countries. Nonetheless, it is necessary to ask, as part of program design, under what conditions one can reasonably expect those structures to coordinate effectively and how bureaucratic incentives can be changed to elicit the required coordination and cooperation.[20] If that is not possible, or at least not initially, it is important to be aware of the trade-offs and to try to minimize them. In the case of Progresa-Oportunidades, strong and direct presidential involvement was essential to achieve the administrative changes described. It was clear to all ministries and agencies that the new program was more than a rhetorical priority of the administration and that the necessary measures would be taken in practice to try to make it a success.[21] But for the reasons just mentioned, such a solution is not sustainable.

Centralized Program Administration

Progresa-Oportunidades is a centrally run program. The administrative unit in charge of the program is a federal agency that gathers all the relevant data, applies the point system, determines eligibility, issues payments to households, contracts for external evaluations, and coordinates service delivery with other federal ministries and agencies. On the other hand, responsibility for direct provision of health and educational services

20. This issue is not only relevant for governments. International financial institutions may also suffer from lack of internal coordination and a horizontal view of social programs, with implications for the countries that they are trying to aid; see chapter 6.

21. Various observations support this view. Prior to the start of Progresa-Oportunidades there were eight Cabinet meetings with the president to analyze and discuss the program; budgetary reallocations proposed by the Ministry of Finance for programs related to Progresa-Oportunidades were continually reviewed by the president; personnel changes were effected at some ministries and agencies; the first head of the newly created unit to administer the program had previously been a direct assistant of the president; the Finance Ministry reported continually to the president on the program's evolution; and so on.

resides with state governments.[22] The overall responsibility for health and educational services for program beneficiaries lies with the federal health and education ministries, respectively, which design and implement the necessary coordination mechanisms with states. As mentioned, the federal resources for health and education services are independent of the program's budget, and they are transferred to state governments through separate channels.

Centralized administration therefore refers to the normative and key operational aspects of the program and to the management of funds transferred to poor households, not to service provision. Since the purpose of the program is to ensure that all poor families in Mexico, regardless of their place of residence, receive the same benefits and are subject to the same eligibility requirements, it was essential to standardize selection criteria and to apply program rules consistently throughout the country. From this point of view, Progresa-Oportunidades should be thought of as a kind of social security program. In many countries, including Mexico, social security transfers are generally carried out by one federal agency that maintains a unified system of administrative records, applies the same nationwide criteria for determining eligibility and the size of benefits, and runs a single payment mechanism.

It is useful to describe briefly the program's operation, particularly the mechanism for making payments to households. Figure 4-2 provides a stylized description of the process. The federal administrative unit determines eligibility after applying the point system to individual household surveys. Once beneficiaries have been incorporated into the program, they must register family members with the health clinic and the school to which they are assigned, which is the closest one; that completes program enrollment. Local health and school officials periodically record a household's attendance at clinics and schools, the requirement for which depends on the age and gender of each member. This information is sent every two months to Mexico City (increasingly by electronic methods), where the administrative unit verifies that the family is in the program and that it has complied with program requirements for the previous two months. The unit then calculates the payment, which is based on the

22. The federal government, though the Social Security Institute, also provides health services in marginalized rural communities of some states, covering approximately one-fourth of all Progresa beneficiaries; in addition, it runs programs to complement state-level efforts to improve the quality of health and educational services. But the bulk of educational and health services are provided by the states.

Figure 4-2. *Progresa-Oportunidades Payment Mechanism*

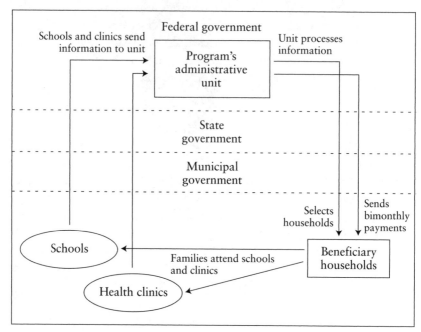

Source: Author's illustration.

number, gender, and school year of children or youth and on the reported attendance of each child at school and of mothers at health clinics. The payment is sent to a payment center, where mothers collect the money and then dispose of it as desired. This procedure is repeated bimonthly; the enrollment information with clinics and schools must be updated each year.

Figure 4-2 highlights an important strength of the program: there are no intermediaries between the federal government and program beneficiaries. That fact helps to limit the opportunities for political manipulation and the possibility of corruption or leakage along the monetary transmission belt, and it reinforces the program's similarity to the program for payment of social security pensions.

But what is seen as a strength by some might be considered a weakness by others. Mexico's social programs, particularly those for poverty alleviation, have a long tradition whereby the relevant authorities (whether the president, a minister, a governor or—why not?—a party official) have a much more direct and visible role in the delivery of benefits. An arm's-length operation like Progresa-Oportunidades runs contrary to that tradition. And because old habits die hard, there is always the risk, and perhaps even the temptation, under different political circumstances to change program operations to correct for the absence of an intermediary. The change might be subtle, but the key point would be to ensure that some authority receives a "thank-you," perhaps required, from beneficiaries.

Put differently, behind the technical details of the way "money flows" lies a central observation: that in the absence of a democratic environment, particularly the checks and balances derived from the active presence of opposition parties, a program like Progresa-Oportunidades could not operate. And insofar as the democratic process weakens, it is perhaps naïve to expect that the weakening will not spill over into a program that benefits one out of every four Mexicans. This observation may be useful when thinking about program replication. Along with the analytical considerations, one needs to consider the political environment in which a program like Progresa-Oportunidades operates, particularly if it is going to be a large-scale program.

A further observation can be made from figure 4-2: there is no community participation in the running of the program. In the past, many programs in Mexico were "community based": for example, the community decided who benefited and who did not and whether to use program money for a school or for roads instead of giving it directly to families. Such programs sometimes lent themselves to manipulation by "local leaders" who often were also party leaders. Without denying the benefits of community participation in other contexts, one can draw a useful analogy with the pension system: nobody calls for community participation in pension programs. These are entitlements that go directly from the government to beneficiaries for their private use, if they fulfill a particular condition (for example, if they were employed for the required number of years in a job with social security benefits). Progresa-Oportunidades transfers are not legally an entitlement, but conceptually they are very similar: an income transfer is given to a family, for its private use, if it has fulfilled particular conditions. Of course, both pensioners and program families might decide to use their resources for a community project—for example, road repair—but that would be a private decision, which must be kept independent from program operation.

Similar remarks apply to what at times is called a "bottom-up" approach to poverty alleviation. Progresa-Oportunidades is not a program built up by poor families and poor communities that decide, according to their perceived needs, how the program should operate and how funds should be used. It is, on the contrary, a "top-down" program, in which all relevant decisions are centrally made. To put it bluntly, poor households have only one decision to make: take it or leave it. And the fact that practically all have decided not only to join but to participate actively and, according to the qualitative evaluations, to feel pride in doing so, might be indicative of a deeper phenomenon: the feasibility of placing income transfer programs for the poor on the same conceptual plane as income transfers for other social groups.

There is one more implication of centralized program operation that is relevant in the context of decentralized service provision. As discussed, state and municipal governments hardly have a say in program operations. From their perspective, this is a federal program, applying federal criteria, funded with federal resources, and operated by federal bureaucrats. They have, in other words, few stakes in Progresa-Oportunidades, although in some poor states up to half of the population might be in the program. Nonetheless, they are supposed to provide, in most cases, the health and educational services needed for program success. True, they have to do this with or without the program. But to the extent that the quality of the services matters to beneficiary households, which it evidently does, absence of state and municipal involvement in the program may diminish its positive impact.

Therefore a potential trade-off exists between centralized program administration and the quality of services received by program beneficiaries. To avoid or minimize the potential trade-off, the federal health and education ministries have special resources in their budgets (aside from those budgeted for the program) to collaborate with state governments and strengthen the quality of services in communities where the program operates. However, results depend on the extent to which officials from the federal health and education ministries pursue quality control as part of their agenda with state governments and on the commitment of individual state governments to poverty alleviation, rhetoric aside. Experience so far shows that results vary across time and place and that they are not always as good as they could be given the budgetary resources allocated to the task.[23]

23. An important task for future evaluations is to present, if the data allow, state-level results—not only nationwide results, as has been the case so far—and to attempt to measure

To sum up: in the case of Progresa-Oportunidades, centralized operations have helped to insulate the day-to-day running of the program from political pressures by state or municipal governments to change eligibility criteria, operations, or the size of benefits (because conditions in their state are "special"). Central administration has been equally essential in keeping operating costs low, allowing most of the program's budget to translate into direct benefits for the poor and not into salaries and administrative expenses for large bureaucracies. It has also contributed to reducing the number of decisionmakers, keeping the program manageable, and it has helped to minimize corruption. And, finally, it has permitted an arm's-length operation that changes the political nature of income transfers for the poor.

Yet those outcomes have not occurred without costs, to the extent that some relevant actors for the success of the program—state governments—are not stakeholders in the program in any real sense, and to the extent that the federal health and education ministries might shirk their program-related tasks, despite having the resources to perform them (particularly if, as mentioned, they gain little politically by performing them). And, perhaps for some, there also have been costs because the previous basis for forming political alliances has been undermined.

On balance, this modus operandi has allowed Progresa-Oportunidades to function. Further, one could argue that without a centralized operation there would be no program today, given the program's departure point and the need to overcome historical inertia. But that is not to say that the program could not function better or that its institutional arrangement would best suit other countries. Whether to centralize operations, like other questions, is best decided on a case-by-case basis.

Transparency, Accountability and Credibility

Progresa-Oportunidades began in the context of Mexico's democratic transition, which may be said to have begun in the mid-1990s, when many reforms were undertaken to change the electoral apparatus and ensure fair elections, limit sources of money for parties, fully open up the

---

the extent to which the quantity and quality of health and educational services affect program outcomes. The effects of variations in the quantity and quality of services are partially captured by the operational evaluations, but so far those effects have not been systematically linked with the quantitative impact evaluations.

media, and so forth (although, as with any major political change, there had been many earlier advances). Since then there has been a lot more political plurality in Congress, state governments, and, as of 2000, the presidency. Mexico's increasingly democratic environment has contributed decisively to the program's strength and continuity. A few weeks prior to the program's official launch in August 1997, the mid-term federal elections produced a lower house of Congress in which no political party had a majority.[24] Because approval of expenditures under the federal budget required the consent of political parties besides the president's party, the executive branch faced a new challenge, and substantive changes to the budget were one immediate implication of the new order.[25] For the purposes of Progresa-Oportunidades, three changes merit special attention: increased transparency, more accountability, and reduced discretion in the execution of social programs financed with federal funds.[26]

Up to the mid-1990s, detailed information on social programs was not easily obtained. In particular, there was insufficient transparency on the criteria for selecting beneficiaries for targeted programs; rules for distributing federal resources between states and municipalities; and the beneficiaries of each program. Equally, there was little or no measurement of the effectiveness of each program's operations, and there were few impact evaluations—and no legal obligation to make the results public when they were conducted. On the whole, ministries and agencies had ample discretionary powers in the administration of social programs and oversight was loose. This situation limited the credibility of program results, particularly with members of Congress who did not belong to the president's party. Without necessarily being true (or at least not always true), accusations would at times be made that some social programs were subject to political manipulation to benefit the party in power; that they had

24. Up to that point, the PRI had had a majority in both houses of Congress for more than seventy years. In the 2000 elections it also lost its majority in the Senate, as well as the presidency.

25. Unlike most constitutional regimes, Mexico has an asymmetric budgetary review process: while both houses of Congress must approve revenues, only the lower house approves expenditures.

26. Other changes involved legal reforms to allocate federal funds to states and municipalities; rules limiting discretion in the allocation of unexpected revenues; elimination of funds not subject to audit; full disclosure of salaries and benefits of federal personnel; and limits on resources available for wage increases for the federal bureaucracy, among others. Some of these measures had started in previous years, but they accelerated rapidly after the change in the composition of Congress. See Levy (2000) for a discussion.

a "clientelist" or "corporativist" bias favoring groups that were not truly needy but were better organized (particularly in urban areas); and that social programs exchanged their benefits for political favors, especially during elections.

Since 1998 the federal budget has included specific provisions to help remedy the situation. The budget decree, focusing on Progresa-Oportunidades, now contains provisions related to transparency, access to information, impact and operational evaluations, and audit mechanisms. Aside from those provisions, the decree obligates the executive branch to issue operational rules, which are detailed regulations that govern the most relevant aspects of the program: amount of cash transfers and in-kind benefits for each member of the household; criteria for selecting beneficiaries, including the household data that must be collected and processed and the confidentiality rules applied to the means-testing procedures (the point system); the rights and obligations of beneficiaries and conditions under which they can continue to participate in the program; criteria for choosing localities; and criteria for making information public, among others. The operational rules, in other words, substantially reduce the discretion of program operators in the process of beneficiary selection, which had been subject to strong criticism in the past.

The operational rules also serve to coordinate the activities of ministries and agencies participating in the program, specifying their obligations and listing the geographical points at which services (health talks, nutritional supplements, educational and health services) must be provided. The rules also specify the information that ministries and agencies must provide to the program's administrative unit to ensure smooth operations.[27]

It is probably fair to say that the operational rules go beyond the requirements established by Congress in the budget decree and, at least in the early years of Progresa-Oportunidades, represented an important milestone in the management of a social program in Mexico. It also is worth noting that compliance by program operators with the rules is subject to external evaluation, to supervision by the Ministry of the Comptrollership, and to potential sanction by Congress's audit office.

The importance of the provisions of the budget decree and the operational rules, however, goes beyond facilitating program operation and

27. The operational rules are signed by the heads of the ministries and agencies participating in the program, and they are published in Mexico's Federal Register and on the program's Internet site.

agency coordination: the provisions have contributed decisively to the continuity of the program by ensuring the transparency of program operations, the accountability of program administrators, and the credibility of program impact and operational indicators.[28]

From a broader perspective, the changes in the composition of Congress, themselves a reflection of a deeper political transition toward an increasingly democratic society, have gradually generated conditions for a more open and informed discussion of public policy in general and of poverty programs in particular. Increased participation by Congress in the discussion has been an indispensable development. When single-party rule and a strong president prevailed, policy discussions took place mainly within the executive branch. Convincing the president of the necessity of a particular course of action was generally sufficient to start a new program or to modify the scope of an existing one, particularly in matters of poverty alleviation, where the interests of powerful groups (for example, large business or trade-union organizations) were not directly affected. In turn, the president's backing meant almost automatic funding by Congress.

But when the president's party does not have a majority in Congress, it is no longer sufficient (although still necessary) to have the support of the president for a new program, even if its technical merits are high. Backing by Congress is essential. But to make an informed decision, Congress must have access to credible information about the program's operations and results and sufficient assurance that it will not be used for other purposes.[29] That is why transparency, accountability, and credibility, the modus operandi of Progresa-Oportunidades, have played such a key role in the program's continuity. Political change in Congress created both an opportunity and a new requirement: an opportunity because, given the lessons of the past, it was clear that the program's continuity over the medium term could be hoped for only if its operations were different from those of previous programs; a requirement because ensuring transparency and accountability was a legal obligation, not the product

28. These indicators should be interpreted in a broad sense: results of the impact evaluations; lists of beneficiaries; operational indicators concerning nutritional supplements distributed, cash payments made, health talks delivered, and so forth; financial information; and the like.

29. Having access does not guarantee that Congress will do so, and congressional institutions designed to analyze the government's programs and projects need to be strengthened as part of the country's democratic transition.

of the president's goodwill or the intentions of the program's designers and administrators. Though difficult in the beginning, the program's modus operandi has strengthened the program. In retrospect, Progresa-Oportunidades was lucky to develop in the context of Mexico's democratic transformation.

On the other hand, it must be noted that the phaseout of the previous food subsidy programs, particularly the long-standing tortilla subsidy, was not the product of a congressional vote; as discussed, it resulted from an administrative decision. While Progresa-Oportunidades was being designed, analysis of the distributional impact of the tortilla subsidy; of its relative ineffectiveness in combating poverty and channeling income to the poor; and of the large arbitrage opportunities that it created, favoring a few, was made available to members of Congress and to the general public. That information tried to convey the message that, rhetorical considerations aside, the subsidy was not the best way to spend public money and that many of the supporters of the subsidy were speaking only for the entrenched interests that had long benefited from it. The new openness contributed to facilitating the decision to phase out the tortilla subsidy, which at the time many considered to be politically very sensitive (as has been the case in other countries).[30] It remains an open question whether, particularly at the beginning of Progresa-Oportunidades, Congress would have voted to eliminate it and the bread subsidy.

The above comments should not be interpreted to mean that a more democratic political context necessarily guarantees that a good program will continue and a bad one will be phased out. That is too strong a statement, and there is insufficient evidence to back it. The point here is only that a more democratic environment usually is associated with stronger or more stable mechanisms to promote transparency and accountability and, almost by definition, to foster open discussion of public policies. Such an environment might, in turn, be more likely to reduce the probability of arbitrary or erratic decisionmaking than one in which political power is much more concentrated.[31] If a program is "good" and that fact

30. During the administration of President de la Madrid (1983–88) an attempt was made to phase out the generalized tortilla subsidy and to replace it with a new tortilla subsidy targeting the urban poor. Nonetheless, it was not possible to phase out the generalized subsidy at that time, and both subsidies coexisted until they were replaced by Progresa-Oportunidades.
31. In addition, generally speaking the larger the program, the greater its visibility and therefore the attention given to it by Congress and the media. After operating more than eight years and providing coverage for one of every four Mexicans, Progresa-Oportunidades

is widely known, then the program is more likely to be insulated from short-run considerations and allowed to continue; if it is "bad," then it is more likely that it can be phased out (particularly if a better substitute is proposed).[32]

These remarks take on particular importance in the case of poverty programs. At least in some countries, including Mexico, the poor are too dispersed and insufficiently organized to form a constituency with sufficient power in Congress to defend a program and ensure its continuity. Democratic elections may be characterized by the overrepresentation of some groups, notably large to medium-size agricultural producers, trade unions, business interests, and public sector workers. The extremely poor are rarely among those groups. Yet the general rhetoric of all political parties in favor of poverty alleviation creates conditions that favor programs like Progresa-Oportuniades. Credible and widely available information increases the probability that legislators will make informed decisions, because it makes it costly for them or members of the executive branch to change course without good reason. In the case of Progresa-Oportunidades, transparency, accountability, and the credibility of the program's indicators have been sufficient so far and have served to align the incentives of the executive branch and Congress in favor of program continuity.[33]

From a different perspective, Progresa-Oportunidades can be seen as a particular case in which the institutional design of a poverty program (interpreted broadly, including its modus operandi) adapted to changing political circumstances and benefited from them. In other countries, circumstances are surely different, imposing different requirements on the institutional design of conditional cash transfer programs. The most useful observation here might simply be to note the need to make explicit these institutional aspects of program design and to incorporate them

---

may have achieved sufficient importance to avoid arbitrary decisionmaking. But such protection is gained only after a program has been in existence for some time; in the early stages the protection coming from sheer size is not present and it is necessary to rely almost exclusively on the transparency, accountability, and credibility of the program's operations.

32. Of course, it is unlikely that there will be unanimous agreement on which programs are good or bad. But a context that encourages open discussion can contribute to presenting empirical evidence on program costs, benefits, and evaluations and permit the gradual emergence of a consensus.

33. There is, of course, no guarantee that that will continue to be the case. In Mexico, the democratic interplay between Congress and the chief executive is less than a decade old, and even substantially more mature democracies may make mistakes, at least in hindsight.

from the beginning because, at a particular future juncture, their contribution to program continuity might be indispensable.

Protection from Electoral Pressures

Congress's role in Progresa-Oportunidades has also contributed to its continuity in yet another way: it has established strong legal provisions against the "political" use of the program. More particularly, it has sought to separate the program from the public image of the president and to provide information directly to beneficiaries about the nature of the benefits that they receive, their rights, and their obligations. Two factors deserve special attention.

First, new provisions in the federal budget decree prohibited using the program in proselytizing by any political party. Since 1998, all documents, materials, and forms that are given to participating households when they receive any benefits have been required to include the following text:

> We remind you that your participation in Oportunidades and receipt of benefits are in no way subject to affiliation with any specific political party or to voting for any specific candidate running for public office. No candidate is authorized to grant or withhold benefits under the program. Eligible beneficiary families will receive support if they show up for their doctor's visits and health education talks and if their children attend school regularly. Any person, organization, or public servant that makes undue use of program resources will be reported to the competent authority and prosecuted under applicable legislation.

Furthermore, the budget decree declared that for program staff,

> Subjecting social programs to electoral or political requirements is a federal offense punishable by law. No public servant may use his or her position or resources to influence votes for or against any specific party or candidate. Oportunidades is a public initiative and the granting or continuation of program benefits does not depend on political parties or candidates.[34]

34. From the annual federal budget decree; author's translation.

The second factor is provisions introduced in the 2000 and 2003 budget decrees prohibiting inclusion of new beneficiaries in the program in the first six months of those years because presidential and mid-term elections, respectively, were held in July of each year.[35]

These two factors contribute to increasing the perception that Progresa-Oportunidades is a politically neutral program and to reducing political parties' concern that the program might be used against their electoral interests. And although those factors might be insufficient to fully align all political parties' incentives in favor of the program, they at least eliminate a reason to be strongly against it. Clearly, such strong legal provisions enhance the credibility of the government's commitment to restrain from political use of the program, facilitating a favorable vote by Congress in each year's budget discussions; such a vote is further facilitated by the fact that Congress has never been asked for an explicit tax increase or a major reduction in other programs to fund Progresa-Oportunidades. These factors, along with the program's positive results, have contributed to the program's transit through three shifts in the composition of the House of Representatives since 1998.[36]

Information and Participation Mechanisms

Since its inception Progresa-Oportunidades has sought to provide information about the program to participants, to Congress, to the academic and policy research community, and, in general, to any interested party. A large amount of information has been easily accessible since the program

35. The 1997 decree did not carry such provisions, but the federal government decided to wait until after the elections were over to start the program although it could have been started in January of that year. Mid-term elections were held in July, and the program was launched in August; the delay increased the government's credibility. During the time that the program was being designed, government officials held informal talks with legislators. Many of them expressed their concern that the program would be "Zedillo's Pronasol" (in reference to a program associated with President Salinas) and that a program that "gives money to the poor" would never be accepted by Congress. Curiously, the provisions prohibiting incorporation of beneficiaries in the first six months of 2006 were not included in the 2006 budget decree.

36. From 1998 to 2006 a specific article on Progresa-Oportunidades was incorporated in each year's budget decree, with the proposed budget and the regulatory provisions just mentioned. It is noteworthy that in all those years no party has specifically voted against that article, nor has the president's proposal ever been modified by Congress. (In Mexico's voting procedures any party or any member of Congress can vote against any individual article of the budget decree.) Over the course of those years three different legislatures have been elected.

began; the program's Internet site contains most of the information mentioned above.[37] In addition, results of the impact and operational evaluations are made public and discussed with the relevant congressional committees. Program administrators regularly attend congressional hearings and inform academics, journalists, and other interested parties of the contents and functioning of the program through seminars, lectures, and talks held throughout the country. Over the years, the program has gained visibility, including at times coverage by foreign newspapers and journals, and it has been the subject of discussion by development agencies.[38] Presentations on the program also have been made at the request of various foreign governments.

With regard to Congress, an effort also was made to identify all poverty programs and projects in the federal budget. Many federal ministries and agencies participate in this task. However, traditionally only spending by the Ministry of Social Development was considered spending on poverty. There was no systematic identification or quantification of programs and budget funds allocated by other institutions for the same purpose. Hence, since 1996, as Progresa-Oportunidades was being designed, the president's budget proposal to Congress has included a quantification and description of all programs comprised by the poverty alleviation strategy. The aim was to evaluate federal efforts as a whole and to identify the many agencies involved and their individual efforts. Doing so enriched budget discussions within the executive branch and the House of Representatives, complementing each ministry's vertical approach with a horizontal view of all federal programs with the same objective. Achieving greater clarity in conveying budget information was important to get across three basic messages in a context of tight budgetary constraints and fierce competition for funding: that resources needed to be allocated for a program to develop the human capital of the

37. See www.oportunidades.gob.mx.
38. Early references include J. Friedland, "Signs of Progresa: Mexico Tries to Take Politics out of Welfare and Focus on the Neediest," *Wall Street Journal,* October 15, 1999; Richard Chacon, "Mexico Turns to Welfare to Aid Poorest," *Boston Globe,* November 1, 1999; Gary Becker, "'Bribe' Third World Parents to Keep Their Children in School," *Business Week,* November 22, 1999. More recent references include Alan Krueger, "A Model for Evaluating the Use of Development Dollars, South of the Border," *New York Times,* May 2, 2002; "Social Programmes That Are Good for Democracy as well as the Fight against Poverty" and "New Thinking about an Old Problem," *Economist,* September 15, 2005. The program also has been discussed in official World Bank and Inter-American Development Bank publications (see, for example, the "Spotlight on Progresa" in the World Development Report for 2004 (World Bank, 2003, p. 30–31).

poor, who were barely receiving any support; that the funding taken away from existing food programs was being reallocated to others that were more effective; and that the redistributive impact of public spending was being strengthened by allocating more funds for income transfers for the poor.

On the other hand, a decision was made to have the program maintain a low profile with respect to broad public opinion. In the first years caution was exercised, for three reasons: one, in order not to create large expectations among the poor that a transfer program would soon reach all of them since, as mentioned, it was uncertain which budgetary resources would be available and when. Two, because the program was initially questioned on political and ideological grounds, there seemed to be little to be gained from a large public information effort for what was then a small program that might not be continued. And three, because the large public communications campaigns that had at times characterized poverty programs of previous administrations had eventually backfired because the opposition parties believed that the president was using the programs for his own gain, hurting the programs' post-administration continuity.

Thus, the information strategy was three-pronged: first, an unheard-of amount of information was made available to all. Second, information was directly communicated to key actors in Congress, subnational governments, academia, and interested parties. Third, the public information campaign kept a low profile.

It should be noted that since 2004 the third element of the public communications strategy has been modified; during the first six months of 2006 in particular, a public information campaign relying on national television and radio was under way that was substantially larger than previous campaigns. While the first and second motives mentioned above for not conducting such a campaign initially are no longer relevant, the third motive may be. If so, some may question the wisdom of this large public information effort, conducted as it was during the 2006 presidential election campaign, given that someone's undoubtedly good intentions to inform may be interpreted by others as the intention to manipulate.

I end this section with a discussion of the role played by program beneficiaries, wherein the issue is not only access to information, but also direct and continuous participation. Once households are selected into the program, they attend talks by program operators on the purposes of the program, its benefits, and its obligations.[39] Materials describing program details also are distributed to participating households. Within each community some beneficiary mothers are selected and trained to play a more active role in the program, as problem solvers for other beneficiaries.[40] Once in the program, mothers regularly meet at health clinics during the health talks that they are all expected to attend; they also attend bimonthly meetings at the payment points. Informational materials are posted at health clinics and in schools participating in the program; in communities where Spanish is not the first language, materials are translated into indigenous languages.

The point here is that Progresa-Oportunidades not only involves a major effort to inform beneficiaries but that it also requires their continuous participation in different aspects of the program. Participants gradually develop a sense of ownership in the program and a sense that the cash transfers received are the direct result of their constant efforts to ensure that their children go to school and that they themselves and their family members go to health clinics for talks and health interventions. As discussed in chapter 3, requiring active participation contributes to beneficiaries' sense of responsibility, self-fulfillment, and empowerment, which is complemented by the right to dispose of their money freely. Poor households are not receiving a handout; they are actively involved in an effort to overcome the impoverished conditions in which they live.

Complementarities and externalities in nutrition, health, and education were the conceptual basis for establishing program requirements, but another factor was involved. The conditions imposed on beneficiary households convert Progresa-Oportunidades into more than a program that provides cash rather than in-kind income transfers. A growing awareness of rights and responsibilities, if nurtured and sustained over time, is bound to have, if it is not already having, important implications for the relationship between poor households and the powers that be.

39. In rural areas, prior to program enrollment a community assembly is held to review the list of potential beneficiaries in order to incorporate information that might have been missed or erroneously collected in the household surveys and then applied to the point system. This mechanism to correct inclusion and exclusion error helps to provide a sense of fairness regarding who does or does not benefit. However, in very few cases have lists been corrected.

40. These voluntary participants perform simple tasks like informing mothers when payments will be made, what happens when payment forms do not arrive on time or when they are incorrect, what clinic to attend, and the like.

Active participation also may help to modify poor individuals' perceptions of themselves. Gradually, that may help break self-perpetuating patterns of behavior that have existed for many decades, particularly in small and remote rural communities. Generational change, higher incomes, a reduced feeling of precariousness, and a greater sense of achievement may slowly change self-defeating attitudes and expectations; they may even contribute to a change in the sense among many poor people that they belong to a highly unequal society made up of "us and them."

Current statistical techniques used in impact evaluations have difficulties measuring such effects, although qualitative evaluations do provide some evidence of the importance of participation for attitudes and behavior. That is not to say that a single program will produce a radical shift in participants' long-standing habits and views, only that it will contribute to doing so. One can therefore speculate that in the future such a gradual shift in perceptions and behavior will contribute to program continuity. To the extent that direct beneficiaries take a more active role in the program, they may make an unjustified phaseout or dilution of the program or a brazen attempt to distort it for political purposes more difficult.

Transition between Federal Administrations

Making the transition from the administration of President Zedillo to that of President Fox was crucial for Progresa-Oportunidades. In December 2000, when the transition occurred, the program had been in place for three and a half years and covered 2.6 million families, mostly in rural areas. Two factors played a key role in the transition.

First, the results of the first set of impact evaluations, made public after the presidential elections (in July 2000) but before the change of administration (in December), were presented by officials of the outgoing administration directly to President-elect Fox and members of his transition team. Second, the positive opinions about the program held by international financial institutions, particularly the Inter-American Development Bank (IDB) and the World Bank, gave Fox independent and credible confirmation of the information received from the officials of the outgoing administration.[41] These factors probably made a decisive contribution

41. Another factor contributing to continuity might have been that some officials who had been among the key promoters of the program since its inception in 1995 were invited by President Fox to join his administration. Some officials at the Finance Ministry moved to the Mexican Social Security Institute, and some were promoted within the Finance

to three key decisions made in December 2000: first, to continue the program;[42] second, to incorporate 750,000 additional families in 2001; and third, to extend the education cash transfers for three more years to cover high school.[43]

Why did Fox's administration continue with Progresa-Oportunidades? First and foremost, it had a genuine commitment, as did the previous one, to poverty alleviation, so continuing a program that appeared to work well was a natural decision, at least until a better alternative was found. Second, the president and senior members of his team were receiving deserved recognition for their attitude of responsibility and maturity in continuing a program that started before they came to power. Third, the program was gradually acquiring some international visibility.[44] Fourth, the program had not been appropriated by the outgoing president or by the party that had been defeated in the 2000 elections; therefore there appeared to be no political need to change course.[45] Fifth, for the reasons discussed above, continuing with the program did not involve a conflict with Congress. And sixth, although program expansions after 2003 were no longer being financed by the phaseout of generalized food subsidies, the additional budgetary pressures were manageable, particularly given

Ministry, but officials at both continued their direct involvement with the program, since the Finance Ministry and the Social Security Institute are members of the technical committee that oversees the program. Similarly, key personnel in the administrative unit in charge of the program also retained their positions, including, initially, its director. It is difficult to assess how much "actor continuity" contributed to facilitating the transition from one administration to the other; at the least, hopefully, it was not a hindrance.

42. It is difficult to speculate to what extent suspending incorporation of new beneficiary households during the electoral period (January–June 2000) and the program's general low profile during that time also facilitated this decision. Those are subjective considerations. On the whole one could say that the program was not much discussed during the electoral campaigns, nor were many accusations made that the government or the Partido Revolucionario Institucional was using it to influence the outcome of the election.

43. As discussed in chapter 3, that decision was based on results in Schultz (2000a, 2000b), which showed that the scholarships had their largest impact on the transition from primary to secondary school and on the additional enrollment in the latter; those results suggested that a strong impact also could be expected from extending the scholarships for three more years to cover high school.

44. For example, in July 2003 an important event took place in Mexico City. In the presence of President Fox, the media, and policymakers from Latin America, the president of the Inter-American Development Bank, the vice president for Latin America of the World Bank, and the Secretary General of the United Nations Economic Commission for Latin America recognized the importance of Progresa-Oportunidades in alleviating poverty in Mexico and called the program a valuable model for other countries.

45. On the contrary, in March 2002 an announcement to expand the program further was made, and the name of the program was changed from Progresa to Oportunidades.

the stable macroeconomic conditions and strengthening of public revenues that resulted from increases in world oil prices at the time.[46]

Contribution of International Institutions

During 1995 and 1996 both the IDB and the World Bank generously provided technical advice on different aspects of the program. Nevertheless, at that time and during the initial years of program operation, it was not deemed convenient to obtain international financing for the program. In 1996–97 such financing would have added yet one more controversial aspect to what was already a fairly significant change in poverty policy, perhaps giving the impression that the program was the result of a mandate of or an adjustment program agreed upon with international financial institutions.[47]

Five years later, however, different political circumstances allowed modification of that assessment. On one hand, it was obvious that the Fox administration had in no way been involved in any previous negotiations with any international financial institution. On the other, those institutions had an ample supply of highly motivated technical experts who could, in the short run, contribute to the work of the officials of the new administration who were in charge of the program, particularly during the critical initial months. As a result, it was considered beneficial for the continuity of the program to take out a loan with the IDB to support program operations. After discussions held in the course of 2001, a loan for US$1 billion was agreed to in March 2002 for a period of three years, the largest loan for a poverty program made by the IDB at that time. (In 2005 the loan was renewed for US$1.2 billion, for four more years.)

The IDB's role in Progresa-Oportunidades extends substantially beyond development finance, however. Technical experts from the IDB had personal relations with and the trust of officials of both the outgoing

46. Oil prices are not a minor consideration. According to the federal budget decrees for the relevant years, the average world oil price for the Mexican export mix was US$31.36 per barrel over the period 2002–05 and US$19.64 for the five previous years in which Progresa was in operation (1997–2001). Oil rents account for more than one-third of government revenues.

47. As a result of the 1994–95 crisis, Mexico held negotiations with the U.S. government and international financial institutions, particularly the International Monetary Fund, as part of Mexico's short-run macroeconomic adjustment program. The agreements reached were discussed intensely in Congress and in the media during 1995.

and the incoming administration, and that fact helped to further communication and understanding at a time of significant change; recall that President Fox was the first president who did not belong to the Partido Revolucionario Institucional (PRI) in more than seventy years. Since then, IDB personnel have acquired detailed knowledge of the program's objectives and operations, allowing them to contribute to the analysis of specific aspects of the program (for example, how to adapt household surveys and the targeting point system as coverage expanded into larger and more urbanized settings). The IDB has also been a promoter of external evaluations by national and international experts, and it has served as an informal forum in which the program is discussed. In a further and perhaps novel feature, the loan's conditions gave the IDB the possibility of participating in discussion of changes to the operational rules, which, as mentioned, have been a key element of the program. It is probably fair to say that the systematic analytical and operational involvement of IDB personnel in the program has been more important than the loan itself and that their involvement has been very positive indeed. Mutatis mutandis, mechanisms of this sort can be extremely helpful in other countries experiencing similar political transitions, regardless of whether there is a need for external financing.

One might point out, on the other hand, that perhaps international financial institutions have not been as involved as is desirable in promoting the overall consistency of Mexico's broader poverty strategy. They could contribute to that aim, to the extent that funding or technical assistance for programs that overlap with Progresa-Oportunidades is subject to careful review, by ensuring that the other programs are compatible with the aims and functions of Progresa-Oportunidades. In the end, the decision of whether to carry out these new programs will not be theirs, but their analysis of program duplication and their advice on how to avoid it certainly would be useful.

Program Phases and Critical Transition Points

Figure 4-3 identifies six phases in the development of Progresa-Oportunidades, along with critical transition points between some of them. Phase 1 (1995–97) pertains to program conception, discussion, and analysis, and it probably has been the most difficult phase of the program so far. It occupied the first two and a half years of President Zedillo's administration and was characterized by intense Cabinet discussions,

Figure 4-3. *Progresa-Oportunidades: Phases and Critical Points*

Phase					
1	2	3	4	5	6
Cabinet discussion Pilot project	Rural and semi-urban coverage	Semi-urban and urban coverage	Full coverage; end of scale-up	Sustainability	Phase-down
1995–97	1998–2001	2002–04	2005–06	2007–?	?

    ↑   ↑   ↑

    First   Second   Third

   critical   critical   critical

 transition transition   transition

Source: Author's illustration.

given the novelty of the approach and the risks that it entailed. The pilot project belongs to this phase, and, as discussed, it provided essential evidence about the technical feasibility of the proposal. But as long as a pilot project was being carried out in a relatively remote state and discussions were contained within federal ministries and agencies, the risks involved were tolerable and, certainly, controlled.

The first critical transition point for the program occurred in mid-1997. At that point ideas had been explored, technical arguments concluded, and feasibility issues, by and large, settled. A political decision to start the program needed to be made. It was a difficult and risky decision because, first, it signaled the beginning of the dismantling of a long-standing system of food subsidies; second, because giving money to poor mothers, under strict conditions, had never been attempted elsewhere; third, because despite long discussions there was an absence of complete consensus in the Cabinet; and fourth, because it involved a substantive shift in the implementation of poverty policy. The decision clearly could be taken only by the president. The program was at a point where leadership was not merely important, it was critical; indeed, without it there would have been no program.

Phase 2 ran from approximately mid-1997 through the end of 2001. Scale-up took place rapidly. Coverage was basically rural, although toward the end poor households in larger semi-urban localities were enrolled. This phase includes the first year of the administration of President Fox, given the special circumstances surrounding the first transmission of power between a PRI and a non-PRI president. As a result of a political agreement between the president and the president-elect, the budget for 2001 was to a large extent prepared by officials of the outgoing administration. It was not reasonable, and it was technically very hard, for the president-elect's transition team to prepare it; it also was unreasonable for the new administration to fully phase out a program all at once. The outgoing officials, committed to the program since its inception, budgeted the resources necessary to continue it, expanded the scholarship component for three additional years, and added 750,000 families.

A second critical transition point occurred between 2001 and 2002. The first year gave the new administration sufficient time to present the National Development Plan, which included the administration's main social policies and programs. Furthermore, the budget for 2002 was wholly within their domain. A decision on whether to continue Progresa was needed, and again, only the president could make that decision. That decision also was difficult, for three reasons: first, because the first PAN (Partido Acción Nacional) president in Mexico's history wanted to signal a break with the past and continuing with a previous administration's program might not have been interpreted as doing so; second, because even within a series of PRI administrations there was no tradition of program continuity (on the contrary, each new administration generally began its own programs); and third, because there were some in the president's political party who argued against continuity, because from their perspective Progresa-Oportunidades was just one more example of the PRI's paternalistic welfare programs that not only locked the poor in poverty but also were used by PRI candidates against PAN candidates during elections.

March 2002 marked the second transition point, as President Fox announced the continuation and expansion of the program, now named Oportunidades. The name change was both essentially irrelevant and immensely relevant: it was irrelevant because it meant nothing in terms of the substantive content of the program, and it was immensely relevant because it made concrete the political commitment of the administration to a program that was now theirs. Once again, the program was at a point where leadership was not merely important, it was critical; without it there would have been no program. And in fact there was, paradoxically, a break with the past: a program from a previous administration was continued.

Phase 3 (2002–04) also was characterized by rapid scale-up, as coverage expanded from semi-urban areas into large urban areas. Operational improvements and innovations were introduced, while evaluations continued. At the end of this phase there was a major, perhaps historic, achievement: for the first time ever, a single program covered practically the entire population living in extreme poverty in Mexico.

In phase 4 (2005–06), scale-up is no longer an issue; the program's expansion is complete. The focus now lies on consolidating operations and correcting deficiencies. This phase leads to the program's third critical transition point, which probably will occur sometime in the course of 2007 (as, for the same reasons given above, it is unlikely that the federal budget for 2007, drafted in the course of 2006, will eliminate funds for the program at once). At that time, the new administration also will decide whether to continue with Progresa-Oportunidades. Its decision may be facilitated if the program sticks to its core principles for the reminder of the Fox administration. Assuming a positive outcome, the program will enter phase 5 in 2007, when the challenge will be to ensure sustainability long enough to achieve program objectives. This is discussed in the next chapter, as is phase 6, program phaseout.

Summary on Scale-Up and Continuity

The preceding discussion tries to identify the different factors that have played a role in program scale-up and continuity; the discussion that follows presents a general overview of the process. Table 4-3 summarizes the program's development over its first eleven years. The first row identifies the time periods, not necessarily of equal duration, since program design to the present. The second row identifies external events that took place during program scale-up. The third identifies the information that served as input for a given decision by policymakers at each point. The decisions are described in the fourth row, while the fifth records two dimensions of program scale-up (coverage and scope).

The table seeks to convey that scaling-up is a process involving the interplay among external factors (for example, economic crisis, elections, changes in world oil prices), information about the program, and policy decisions made by leaders with given objectives and constraints. In the case of Mexico, the process was triggered by a drastic event: a major economic crisis. As the process began, information became available (regarding, for example, attitudes of beneficiaries and evaluations of the pilot project). That information contributed to changing the political constraints of policymakers (for example, they discovered that substituting targeted food subsidies for conditional cash transfers was well received by poor households). The information also was used to correct operational aspects of the program or to modify its scope (for example, since imposing conditions on beneficiaries was shown to work, officials could consider adding an education component). As scale-up continued, more information became available, allowing other actors to understand the nature of the program better; for example, the program's political neutrality was observed in practice, modifying congressional preconceptions. Improved understanding allowed for further scale-up.

Sooner or later, some actors change (for example, a new president is elected or the composition of Congress changes). If program information is positive, credible, and timely and previous program operation has been reasonably neutral from a political point of view (for example, results of recent external evaluations are good, opinions from multilateral agencies are positive, and there have been no major cases of political manipulation), the new actors may be willing to continue program scale-up. They also may decide to modify the scope of the program or its image (for example, increase benefits by offering high school scholarships, extend coverage to larger urban areas, or change the program's name). The scale-up process is facilitated to the extent that it can tap politically sustainable sources of funding (which may become available, for example, when gradually phasing out generalized subsidies is thought to be feasible, economic recovery continues, or world oil prices rise). Furthermore, as conditions change, additional actors may come into play and contribute to program expansion (for example, multilateral financial institutions may lend money and become actively involved in the program); other factors also may help to maintain incentives favoring the program (for example, increased recognition from the academic and policy community, and greater international visibility).

The scale-up process also is aided by what does not occur: for example, electoral or political manipulation of the program in a large and systematic scale; disruption of family or community relationships; major complaints or criticisms from state or municipal governments; accusations of corruption and fraud; a major economic crisis that forces large budget cuts; or other negative events that might alter the political equilibrium between key actors and decisionmakers.

Table 4-3. *Factors in Progresa-Oportunidades Scale-Up and Continuity, 1994–2006*

Time period	December 1994–September 1995	March 1995–June 1997	July 1997	August 1997–December 1999	January–June 2000
External events	Economic crisis. Start of Zedillo administration.	Economic recovery after September 1995.	Mid-term elections.	Economic recovery continues. Price of oil falls in 1998 but recovers gradually in 1999.	Presidential elections.
Available information	Strong deficiencies in food programs. Little coordination between agencies.	Cabinet discussions on social policy. Positive evaluation results of pilot project.	PRI loses majority in Congress.	Field experience shows that program works and is well accepted.	
Policy decisions	Moderate expansion of existing programs. Start design of alternatives. Start pilot project.	Scale up to three components, adding education. Begin gradual phase-out of generalized food subsidies. Begin Progresa after the mid-term elections.	Centralized operations and creation of new unit to run Progresa. Begin impact evaluation.	Accelerate phaseout of all generalized food subsidies. Continue program expansion. Begin reduction in targeted food subsidies.	Temporary suspension of enrollment of new families in Progresa before elections. Close Conasupo (the tortilla subsidy agency).
Program scale	30,000 households, one state, two components (food and health).	Convert pilot program into Progresa.	300,000 families in 6,344 rural communities in twelve states.	Expansion continues to more states and rural communities and to semi-urban localities.	

July–November 2000	December 2000	January 2001–June 2003	July 2003	August 2003–December 2005	January–June 2006
Fox elected president. No party has a majority in Congress.	President Fox begins mandate.	World recession. Economic slowdown.	Mid-term elections.	Mild recovery in economic growth. Increases in world oil prices.	Presidential elections.
Results of external impact evaluations are available. Progresa is not an issue in presidential elections.	Positive opinion of Progresa held by World Bank and IDB.	Further results of evaluation studies show additional positive impacts. Progresa begins to receive increasing international recognition.	No party gains majority in Congress.	Oportunidades gains international recognition. Evaluation results shows some deficiencies in nutritional component.	Dispute between Congress and the president over public information campaign regarding Oportunidades before elections.
Present evaluation results to president-elect and transition team.	Continue the program.	Progresa's name changed to Oportunidades. US$1 billion dollar loan contracted with IDB.		Change in the type of iron used in nutritional formula. Add a lump-sum payment upon completion of high school.	
Continue expansion to reach 2.6 million families.	Add 750,000 families. Add high school scholarships.	Expansion continues to 4.2 million families and larger urban areas, but enrollment is suspended in January-June 2003 before mid-term elections.		Program reaches 5 million families in December 2004.	Coverage of 5 million families maintained.

None of the forgoing discussion, however, should be interpreted to mean that program scale-up in Mexico has taken place according to an exact, predetermined ten-year plan. That has not been the case. Since the origins of the program in 1995 until today, there has been a process of learning, correction, and adaptation in various dimensions: technical, administrative, operational, and political. Mistakes of many sorts have been made along the way. Some have been corrected; others remain to be fully addressed. Some aspects of the program have not worked as well as planned, and others have been achieved with perhaps more friction and conflict than was necessary. For more than a decade procedures and practices have been adapted in the context of the large social and political changes that are occurring in Mexico. Program designers could not foresee in 1995 and 1996 the substantive changes that occurred in Congress in 1997, even less the outcome of the 2000 elections; nor could they foresee the evaluation results or the evolution of the economy. The ability to adapt strategies and procedures has been central to the program's success.

But while there was no precise ten-year plan, there was a long-term vision and a single objective: to design a technically sound, perhaps innovative, program to redistribute income to the poor while enhancing their human capital; to fund the program in a macroeconomically sustainable way; to implement it in a transparent and politically neutral fashion; to evaluate it systematically and render clear accounts; and to extend its benefits to all of Mexico's poor households. There has been admirable consistency and persistence in this endeavor, a result of the contributions of many participants: two presidents, various members of Congress, senior and mid-level officials from two administrations, national and international academic researchers, advisers and officials from international financial institutions, and, at the center, program beneficiaries, who have shown perhaps the greatest responsibility, consistency, and persistence of all.

Program Replication

Mention has been made of the possibility of replicating some of the program's institutional features in other countries. Although it may seem obvious, it is important to keep in mind that countries are extremely different, and many of those differences affect implementation of a program like Progresa-Oportunidades: size, severity and depth of poverty, urban-rural population distribution, physical infrastructure, political institutions, administrative capacity, level of decentralization of services, and so on. Clearly, it is unlikely that a direct replication of any program developed for one country will succeed in another. There must be a process of adaptation to the specific circumstances in each case; across-the-board application may do more harm than good. Therefore a discussion of program replication is perhaps more useful if it emphasizes general ideas, perhaps broad lessons, derived from the case of Mexico that, mutatis mutandis, might be useful to other countries. Five issues are worth discussing, in addition to the observations made before.

First, it is possible to replace in-kind income transfers (that is, food subsidies) with cash income transfers. For a given budget, replacement will result in more efficiency in reaching the pure objective of augmenting poor households' income, an effect that is larger the more unequal the underlying income distribution. The cash transfer also will be more effective than the in-kind transfer. Moreover, since cash transfers avoid price ceilings, subsidies, and the like, there will be additional efficiency gains from eliminating the dead-weight losses associated with such distortions. Furthermore, since in-kind income transfers may require an administrative apparatus for storing and distributing food (or even producing it) or for supervising and enforcing price subsidies or controls, closing down that apparatus will bring additional gains—and, on occasion, eliminate the opportunities for arbitrage and corruption associated with it. On the other hand, even in very small and remote rural communities the purchasing power associated with cash income transfers need not increase food prices; the supply of food is very elastic. Finally, poor households rarely waste their cash income transfers on cigarettes and alcohol; on the contrary, on the whole they spend their additional resources on basic necessities (mostly food, but not only food), an effect that is reinforced if households receive useful information. In sum, the problem is not access to food, but access to income.

Second, the conditions for receipt of benefits are important. Progresa-Oportunidades is a cash income transfer program that explicitly makes receipt contingent on some behavior that there appears to be a good reason to promote. Food subsidies are an in-kind income transfer program that implicitly makes receipt contingent on some behavior that there appears to be no reason to promote.[48] Progresa-Oportunidades made its conditions explicit, based on one empirical observation and one hypothesis. The observation was that the existence of complementarities among

48. If maize tortillas are subsidized, but bread is not, I receive the income transfer only if I consume tortillas. Yet it is not clear why I should receive an income transfer for consuming tortillas but not for consuming bread (or for consuming tortillas made from wheat, as in the north of Mexico).

nutrition, preventive health care, and basic education indicated that improving them at the same time would create a greater positive impact. The hypothesis is that income transfers subject to the appropriate conditions can gradually augment poor households' assets, particularly their human capital, creating the possibility that the program can eventually be phased out. The point here is that instead of just transferring income (in cash or in-kind), something else should be done to correct the underlying conditions that create the need for these transfers, making it feasible and credible to eventually phase them out. Progresa-Oportunidades is showing that imposing explicit conditions with that purpose in mind is working.

It is important to note, however, that a conditional cash transfer program consists of two separable components: conditions are not an essential component of a cash transfer program, although they most likely are a desirable one. Some countries might want to have just a cash transfer program, either because they see no need for conditions, because conditions cannot be enforced, or because their only goal is to eliminate relative price distortions.[49] Other countries may choose to impose conditions that are quite different from those imposed by Progresa-Oportunidades. For instance, if the school attendance rate among the extremely poor is high, the conditions might apply to performance, not attendance (or a mix of the two, depending on grade level). More generally, imposing conditions adds value to a pure cash transfer program if they promote some socially desirable behavior that would not occur without them. In the case of Mexico's poor, the behaviors that were considered important to promote were attending school and using preventive health services; clearly, desirable behaviors vary from country to country.

Imposing conditions on receipt of benefits may be important for two other reasons. The first, previously mentioned, is that doing so might elicit active participation by poor households, changing the nature of the program from one that could be perceived as giving beneficiaries a handout to one that requires beneficiaries to assume responsibility for trying to improve their circumstances. But the second reason is that it might

---

49. These distortions need not relate to food only. There may be large generalized subsidies for electricity, gasoline, fuel oil, or transportation that need to be trimmed because they weigh heavily in the government budget (or, for example, because there is going to be a trade liberalization process). In that case a targeted cash program might be an effective way to protect the poor; see Dávila and Levy (2003) for a general discussion. Properly used, cash transfer programs might be very useful instruments to compensate for diverse types of shocks.

contribute to the acceptance of the cash transfer program by the general public, given that in some countries a program that "just gives money" to poor families may not be politically acceptable.[50] These two considerations, however, may differ from country to country. Therefore, in determining the conditions of a cash transfer program, social traditions, values, and perceptions must be weighed, in conjunction with the program's impact on incentives and intertemporal asset accumulation.

More generally, Progresa-Oportunidades can be thought of as a particular example of a general class of programs that allow the government to substitute direct transfers for a potentially large set of redistributive instruments based on the price system (subsidies for food, urban transportation, fuels for home cooking, and domestic telephone or electricity rates; VAT exemptions on some goods; and so on). Aside from being more effective in its redistributive objective, the program also allows the government to de-link redistributive considerations from the structure of relative prices, so that those prices and tax rates can be set to maximize economic efficiency and competition in the relevant markets. In addition, this general class of programs can modify the underlying conditions that determine who really benefits from redistribution (and by how much), changing what at times might be rather capricious reasons (place of residence, method of transportation used, type of food items consumed) for other conditions that might contribute more to a given social objective (improvements in education, health, training, and so on).

Yet a third issue has to do with the nature of the program and the population it covers. Although Progresa-Oportunidades was triggered by a short-run economic crisis, its purpose is not to help households that are temporarily living in poverty because of economic fluctuations (or terms of trade or other types of shock). The program focuses on families that are suffering from structural poverty and that need government support even when there are good harvests, no natural disasters, and growth. Of course, other households should receive help if there is an unexpected negative short-run shock, but that is best done through other programs. And, of course, the program can be used to protect households that already suffer from structural poverty (and that presumably are already covered by the program) from the additional negative effects of these

---

50. Consumption subsidies (for food, fuel oil, and so forth) could also be labeled as programs that "just hand out money," but the mechanism is not transparent and generally they are not perceived as such.

shocks. The point here is that setting multiple objectives for a single program will sooner or later lead to confusion. The program will deviate from its objectives and modus operandi, increasing the likelihood that it will end up as a fix-all program subject to increasing political pressures.[51]

Those pressures need not result from pure political expediency alone, however; they may also result from the absence of other programs that can serve to mitigate the short-run effects of unexpected shocks. It is probably unreasonable to expect a government to refrain from using a program like Progresa-Oportunidades to cope with a short-run shock if it has no other instrument available. In the case of Mexico, other instruments were developed to help deal with short-run situations, and Progresa-Oportunidades was protected from political pressures because alternatives were available.[52] Therefore, in thinking about program replication, countries may want to introduce or strengthen other parallel instruments or programs when they consider a conditional cash transfer program. Doing so will increase the probability that the conditional cash transfer program can focus on its medium-term objectives.

A fourth issue relates to evaluation. If for budgetary or operational reasons it is not feasible to completely cover the target population of the program from the start, then a randomized evaluation with treatment and control groups can be set up. However, there will be only a short time for that to occur, perhaps a few months during program start-up, but the opportunity should not be missed. If it is, evaluation will become more difficult afterward, a situation that should be avoided, for two reasons: first, because evaluation is the most objective mechanism for judging whether the program is having its intended effect (along whatever margin of behavior is being pursued) and because it permits early correction of design or operational flaws; second, because evaluation results can be decisive for program continuity, as has been the case in Mexico.

At the same time, care should be taken to avoid "evaluatory capture" of evaluators by program administrators.[53] To the extent that program

51. How would the targeting mechanism work for families that are not poor but suffer a temporary setback from an unexpected shock? Would they also be subject to the same conditions? How long would they be in the program?

52. The Natural Disaster Fund was started in 1996 to replace assets lost by the poor (their harvest, fishing boats, sewing machine, house, and so forth) in such a disaster; temporary employment programs also were promoted; see Levy and Rodriguez (2004).

53. The expression is used here by analogy with the term "regulatory capture," used in the industrial organization literature.

designers and operators consider the future of their program to be tied to evaluation results, they may attempt to influence those in charge of the evaluation to produce particular results or to ignore those that may not be favorable. Although the temptation may vary from country to country, mechanisms need to be implemented to ensure that evaluations are carried out by professionals who have no stake in the program, except for performing a proper evaluation and reporting whatever results are found. Evaluations that are not credible do not help the poor.

Fifth, finally, a program is not a strategy. When contemplating a program similar to Progresa-Oportunidades, government officials should consider how it fits within their country's overall poverty alleviation strategy and within the broader framework of other social programs that transfer income to non-poor households.[54] On one hand, they must establish the total value of the transfers and the conditions of receipt, not only to avoid generating a policy-induced poverty trap (discussed in chapter 1 and elaborated on in the next chapter) but also to facilitate the gradual incorporation of poor households into the set of programs designed to benefit non-poor households. On the other hand, they must avoid the risk that ministries and agencies, in the face of a large-scale, highly visible poverty program, might assume that they have no further responsibilities toward poverty alleviation, since the poor already have been "taken care off" by the program. Poor households in Mexico, and probably in other countries, need more than a program to pull out of poverty permanently.

This section ends with a question. Of all the elements discussed in this chapter, which are the sine qua non for scale-up and continuity? That may be an important question for policymakers, particularly if it is not possible to work on all fronts at the same time. Figure 4-4 attempts an answer. In the center of the figure are the core elements, classified in three groups. First are the technical elements of the program: good microeconomic design, macroeconomically sustainable fiscal resources, reasonably positive response on the supply side, and good technical staff.

---

54. For instance, in some countries (Mexico included), social security programs are financed with government funds in addition to workers' and firms' contributions. Such programs are de facto income transfer mechanisms for those benefiting from social security. Cash transfers from programs like Progresa-Oportunidades should not be established independently of other such transfers, nor should the conditions for one set of programs be independent of others. This issue has yet to be fully addressed in Mexico, in part because despite Progresa-Oportunidades, social policy is still designed with a "vertical" view by ministries and agencies.

Figure 4-4. *Elements of Program Scale-Up and Continuity*

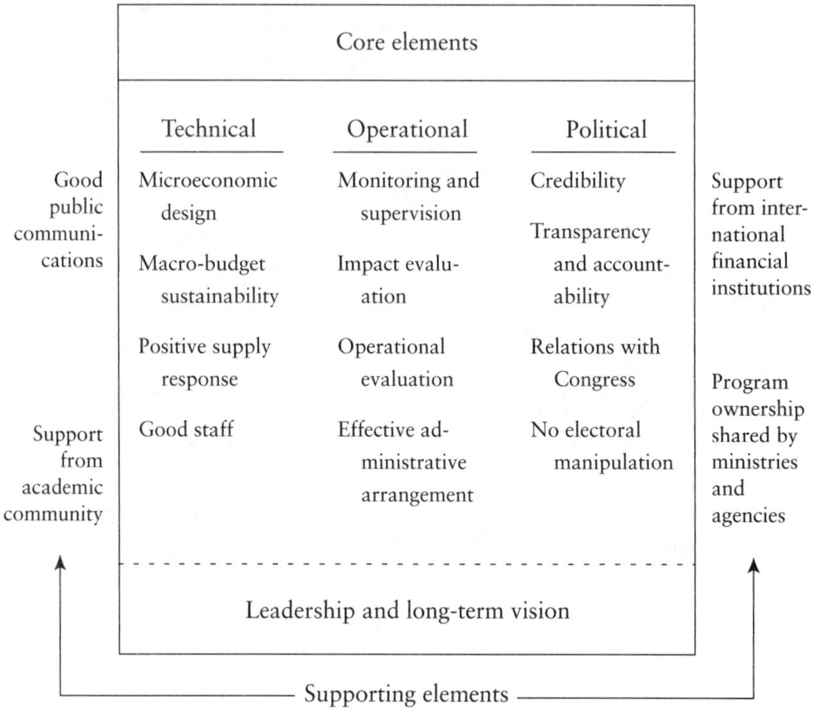

	Core elements		
	Technical	Operational	Political
Good public communi- cations	Microeconomic design	Monitoring and supervision	Credibility	Support from inter- national financial institutions
	Macro-budget sustainability	Impact evalu- ation	Transparency and account- ability	
	Positive supply response	Operational evaluation	Relations with Congress	Program ownership shared by ministries and agencies
Support from academic community	Good staff	Effective ad- ministrative arrangement	No electoral manipulation	
	Leadership and long-term vision		
	Supporting elements		

Source: Author's illustration.

But that is not enough. The second group of core elements is associated with program operation and evaluation. By their nature, these elements become relevant primarily after program start-up: an administrative arrangement that solves the problem of coordinating the activities of ministries and agencies or at least bypasses it; continuous supervision and monitoring of program operations; systematic impact evaluation; and feedback from program evaluation to program design and operation. These elements are essential for continuity, because they determine whether households will in fact benefit from the program and allow actors besides program designers to judge the merits of continuing with the endeavor or not.

But that is not enough either. The third group of core elements is associated with what may be called the program's political operation: its credibility, accountability, and image among members of Congress—in short, whether is it considered "clean," that is, having no direct influence on the electoral process. Without a clean political image, the program will last while the administration that started it is in power, but its chances of survival may diminish rapidly afterward.

It is probably fair to say that in many poverty programs, not only in Mexico but elsewhere, the elements in the first group are the ones that receive the most attention. That is natural, as that is the realm in which most technically minded economists can make a positive contribution (given the incentives of the policymaking environment). But the purpose of putting the other two groups of elements in the same core box (see figure 4-4) is to highlight that this is an all-or-nothing package. All three must be included simultaneously to ensure program continuity. Poverty programs that do not incorporate groups two and three in the initial program design cannot be considered good poverty programs, if the criterion for success is having a lasting impact on a significant share of the country's poor. Perhaps the novelty of Progresa-Oportunidades lies in considering, from the beginning, all the elements in the core box, rather than just some individual elements.

Figure 4-4 places at the bottom of the core box yet another element essential for continuity: political leadership and long-term vision. This component is difficult to measure, but as described before, at critical junctures it has not been simply important, it has been the sine qua non of program start-up and continuity. It is the responsibility of program designers and administrators to ensure that all three groups of elements in the core box are tackled appropriately; it also should be their responsibility to try to create consensus among all parties involved and facilitate decisions to start, scale up, and sustain a program. But at the end of the day, these will not be their decisions. Political leadership need not be there all the time, but it must be there at critical points in time.

Other elements of program scale-up and continuity are certainly important and clearly desirable but probably not essential. Figure 4-4 lists four: shared program ownership by relevant ministries; good public communications; support from international financial institutions; and involvement of the academic community. It helps if all ministers are on board, but if for whatever reason that is not the case, strong political backing from the president might be enough (trade-offs notwithstanding). It also helps if the media are behind the program from the beginning, but with sufficient political support and a clear purpose, the program may be able to do without it. It is useful, at appropriate moments, to have the support of international financial institutions and even to use them as a resource in designing a program or ensuring its continuity, but if they are not there the program can develop nevertheless; the same applies to academic experts. In a nutshell, one could argue that so far Progresa-Oportunidades has ensured that all the elements in the core box are present and at times has had the benefit of some of the elements outside it.

CHAPTER FIVE

Program
Perspectives

Progresa-Oportunidades faces significant future chal-
lenges. Three of them pertain to the program itself: the need for consistency
and sustainability, the need for continuous evaluation, and the need for
long-term institutional stability. The fourth is a different challenge, substantially overlooked so far: how to ensure that Progresa-Oportunidades
fits in with other social programs so that together they provide the right
incentives for poor workers to search for more productive jobs and earn
higher incomes through their own efforts.

Need for Consistency and Sustainability

Table 5-1 presents the age and gender distribution of all Progresa-Oportunidades beneficiaries at the close of 2005. It also identifies, in the relevant age ranges, those with or without a program scholarship. Four
observations can be made. First, the program had 24,066,542 beneficiaries, of whom 51.3 percent were women; nonetheless, in the range of
twenty-two to forty-five years of age, there were almost 16 percent more
women than men. That is an important difference in the gender composition of that population segment, and its medium-term demographic and
social implications deserve more study. One is tempted to attribute the
difference to migration, with men in that age range migrating more than
women, but more analysis is needed to assert that as fact.

Table 5-1. *Age and Gender Distribution of Progresa-Oportunidades Population*

Age group	Population		With scholarship		Without scholarship	
	Men	Women	Men	Women	Men	Women
0–5	871,394	856,237	—	—	871,393	856,233
6-10	1,689,146	1,660,282	781,253	807,452	907,893	852,830
11	389,297	383,743	342,908	343,971	46,389	39,772
12	394,969	390,420	340,769	338,314	54,200	52,106
13	397,641	392,097	329,967	324,217	67,674	67,880
14	385,865	380,635	296,163	294,243	89,702	86,392
15	376,109	372,276	220,208	218,719	155,901	153,557
16	345,987	342,641	148,531	154,134	197,456	188,507
17	325,802	325,893	101,990	111,595	223,812	214,298
18	306,163	307,834	44,105	44,521	262,058	263,313
19	290,545	297,337	17,318	16,241	273,227	281,096
20	262,417	271,257	6,508	6,214	255,909	265,043
21	241,870	256,191	2,488	2,555	239,382	253,636
22–45	3,530,564	4,081,972	—	—	3,530,130	4,081,443
46–59	994,798	1,051,346	—	—	994,798	1,051,342
60–69	454,288	487,136	—	—	454,288	487,135
70 or more	459,894	488,541	—	—	459,894	488,541
Age not specified	1,917	2,038	—	—	1,917	2,038
Total	11,718,666	12,347,876	2,632,641	2,662,700	9,086,023	9,685,162

Source: Author's compilation with data from the National Coordinating Agency for the Human Development Program Oportunidades.

Second and equally important, there were 11.8 million beneficiaries in the working-age range, say eighteen to sixty years of age (not all of them, of course, active in the labor market). With very few exceptions, those people had not been beneficiaries of program scholarships, and most of them did not finish their basic education. As noted in chapter 3, the program has had very little impact on the reenrollment rates of those who abandoned school three or more years before the program started in their community. Given the rate at which the program was scaled up over the course of 1997–2005, those people were, so to speak, not within the program's reach (particularly since the high school scholarships started only in 2001 and then only gradually). For them to have benefited directly from having had more years of education, the program would have had to have started one or two decades before. As that was not the case, these generations of poor workers with hardly any education will be in the labor force for two more decades on average, and many for three or four.

Third, the educational impact of Progresa-Oportunidades is more pronounced among children of younger ages. Among young people aged sixteen to twenty-one years, more are out of school than in school.[1] From the age of fifteen and less, the number of young people in school exceeds that of those out of school, with the proportion increasing with lower ages (remember that program scholarships start at the third year of primary school, so for children under ten years of age, not having a scholarship is not an indication of not going to school). Fourth, finally, there are 1.7 million children aged zero to five years who will begin their schooling in 2006 or later and who will require approximately eighteen years more to complete high school. (Obviously, more children will be born in the years ahead, extending the cycle.)

These observations have two purposes. First, although Progresa-Oportunidades has now been fully scaled up, in that practically all poor families in Mexico are in the program, the number of poor people who will not benefit directly from the program's educational component is still very large. At present, the proportion of beneficiaries who are in the labor market and have benefited from a program scholarship is insubstantial. That proportion will increase gradually, until eventually all workers in the labor force have completed their high school education (hopefully). The point is that it will take a long time for this transition to work itself out. It is wrong to think that just because the program is now fully scaled up, the problem of school attendance among poor youth has been taken care of, let alone the problem of the quality of the education that they receive. Clearly, most poor workers today need other programs and policies, aside from Progresa-Oportunidades, to improve their education and life-time income.

The second purpose concerns the program itself. Hopefully, over the next decades Mexico will experience higher rates of economic growth than in the past. But experience shows that even if it does, it takes a long time for GDP growth to be reflected in growth in the income of the poor. Realistically, many poor households will still need the program's income transfers if their children are to complete high school. If rapid economic growth does not occur, the need may be more pressing still. In any event, if the 9.4 million children and young people aged fifteen years or less who

1. For this age range it is assumed that not having a scholarship implies not being enrolled in school. It is unlikely that a family that is in the program and has a child going to school will not claim a scholarship for that child.

are in the program today (plus those born in the next few years) are to eventually enter the labor force with at least a high school education, in all likelihood they will need Progresa-Oportunidades for a good number of years.

The issue can be put differently: the demographic dynamics of poor households creates a need for long-term support. If the policy objective is to ensure that all poor children today complete their high school education two decades hence, then it will probably be necessary to have the program in place for a long time. It need not be two decades, but perhaps at least one decade more. Constant measurement and evaluation are required to assess how much progress is made over time (with, obviously, the necessary adjustments to the program's incentive structure as results of future evaluations become available). At the same time, the program need not always continue at its current scale; over time, a greater proportion of program families should replace their transfers with their own earned income.

A similar argument can be derived from health indicators, although in this case it is not possible to illustrate in table 5-1 the magnitude of the lags, as was done with education. But the point is the same: basic health and nutrition indicators for poor households are still substantially behind those of non-poor households. Progresa-Oportunidades is helping to narrow the differences, but it has not eliminated them yet. There are still undernourished children who need supplements, mortality rates are still higher than for the non-poor, and so on. Even if a precise number cannot be given, there will be a need for the program for many additional years, on health and nutrition grounds as well as on educational grounds. As with education, constant measurement and evaluation is needed to assess the need.

Program sustainability, therefore, is essential. The issue is no longer scale-up; as mentioned, that is complete. Neither is the issue access to budgetary resources; as GDP grows, the program's share of the federal budget and of GDP will decrease. Nor is the issue technical capability— ten years after program start-up, the know-how is there, notwithstanding improvements that can be incorporated in the future. Ensuring sustainability is a key challenge.

A second key challenge is conceptual consistency: sticking to the program's objectives. With a large-scale program in place, there might be a temptation to use it for purposes for which it was not designed. Adding more objectives or more components to Progresa-Oportunidades is risky, for at least three reasons: first, because as program scope increases, the attention given to current tasks inevitably decreases; the program may be doing more things, but it is more likely to be achieving less altogether. The program's objectives already are ambitious, and its operations complex; it is enough to continue to try to achieve its existing objectives (and, if possible, to do a better job of it). Second, chapters 3 and 4 pointed out many issues with the program that need to be properly addressed. Adding more components before that is done will almost certainly reduce the impact of the program.

The third reason is more powerful. Adding more benefits or objectives to the program without considering how they fit with other social programs will do more harm than good. In particular, extreme care is required to ensure that program benefits do not interfere with workers' decisions to participate in the labor market or with their search for jobs in the "informal" or "formal" segment of the labor market. The program's benefits were designed to expire before beneficiaries begin to seek jobs. Overlapping program benefits with the benefits that workers get depending on their form of participation in the labor market will significantly distort workers' and firms' employment decisions.[2] The short-run political gain that could be obtained from adding more benefits would come, as it did so often in the past, at the cost of long-term social and economic improvement.

Yet a third key challenge is operational consistency. If Progresa-Oportunidades is to continue to enhance the human capital of the poor, its conditions for participation must be systematically enforced. But it is easy, with the passage of time, to overlook that need. The program's administrators need to ensure that participating children attend school and that school teachers and officials do not simply send forms to Mexico City certifying that those children have done so when they actually have not. The same pertains to attendance at health clinics. If enforcement

---

2. It is from this angle that the recent proposal to add a capitalized pension scheme for workers in program families that are currently in the labor force needs to be evaluated. It is extremely unlikely that the scheme is a good idea, and it is an almost complete certainty that it will damage the long-term interests of poor workers (this without even considering its financing). This issue is different from supporting program households that today are made up only of old people who no longer participate in the labor market. In the latter case it is a question about the appropriate combination of the food component and the educational component. Thought can be given to changing the balance of components for households that currently include older people. But, semantics aside, these additional transfers are not pensions.

of conditions weakens, the program runs the real risk of becoming just a mechanism for effecting pure income transfers to the poor: today's consumption is enhanced, but tomorrow's potential is wasted. But operational consistency cannot depend permanently on administrators' good intentions: external auditing mechanisms are required. Experience suggests that without external checks and balances, operational consistency will erode sooner rather than later. Ensuring consistency is important to the extent that, by and large, external auditing mechanisms have so far centered on the good use of resources and the selection mechanisms for localities and families. That focus was understandable given past practices and given the need for building program credibility on those key dimensions. But as the program moves on, the focus of external auditing and supervision needs to adapt as well.

There is, finally, a fourth key challenge: consistency in the poverty strategy. As discussed, ensuring strategic consistency has proven to be substantially more difficult than ensuring program consistency, and strategic consistency has not really been present all along. Compared with the situation a decade ago, there is greater awareness that a strategy is not the arithmetical sum of many programs. But that awareness has yet to be fully reflected in policy design and implementation. This issue goes beyond Progresa-Oportunidades but affects it. The effectiveness of a scaled-up, sustained, operationally consistent, systematically evaluated, and sharply focused program—which is what Progresa-Oportunidades must become in the future—can be diminished in an environment in which other programs operate in different directions, distort incentives, and send confusing signals to all.

Need for Continuous Evaluation

Evaluation, as an integral component of the program, needs to continue. Two broad sets of challenges emerge. One is technical in nature and consists of two parts. The first relates to the systematic data-gathering process, which has been the sine qua non of all the evaluation efforts. Persistence here is indispensable, as researchers follow successive cohorts of program beneficiaries with household surveys and interviews as well as compile data from health clinics and schools. In fact, even more data will be required in the future, particularly on the transition from high school to the labor market and other productive activities.

The second part derives from the increasing difficulty of relying on a randomized approach to construct treatment and control groups. Ignoring exclusion errors, program coverage is now slightly larger than the population estimated to be in extreme poverty in Mexico. Therefore practically all poor households are now in the treatment group, and experimental design methods can no longer be used to measure the program's impacts. Future evaluations increasingly will need to rely on "quasi-experimental design" methods, as is the case with the more recent studies reported in chapter 3.

The second set of challenges concerns issues that need to be addressed, and it too consists of two parts. First, it is essential to continue evaluating the program's fulfillment of its basic objectives. If the program is sustained because health, nutritional, and educational deficiencies in poor households persist, then officials need to know whether, after initial improvements, those deficiencies continue to be reduced. Given the results so far, this is no longer a new issue, but it is still the central issue. To continue with the program without testing its effectiveness is to revert to the problems that it was meant to overcome.

The second part relates to new issues that have arisen given the current stage of the program. Three are discussed here. First, while children and youth are going to school more and may be performing better, little is known about the quality of education that they are acquiring. Going to school is not the sole input in attaining a better education. Research is required to ascertain whether, given the quality of schools, learning by program students is sufficient or whether stronger incentives should be added to the program by, for example, making scholarships contingent on performance as well as attendance. It also may be that schools in program localities are of lower quality than other schools in Mexico and that those schools need to be reinforced by other programs to bring them up to national standards. In sum, given that larger numbers of poor children and youth now attend school, research and evaluation are needed to guide policy on how to ensure that higher attendance translates into improved education.

A second issue concerns the post–high school transition for youth who have benefited from program scholarships. Consider, for example, the ten-year-olds who entered the program when it began in 1997 and now are eighteen or nineteen years old. Assuming that they continued in school, they have already finished or will soon finish high school. (They will be, so to speak, the first generation of fully supported students.) Will these young people pursue a college education, join the labor market, start a microbusiness, or migrate abroad? Are their choices being affected by the program? If they enter the labor market, is their higher education translating into an increased probability of finding a job in the formal segment of the market or a better-paying job? If they start a microbusiness, is the probability of its success increased by the previous or current benefits of the program? Or is Progresa-Oportunidades, sadly, just financing an improved labor force for the United States?

Third, as time passes, more and more families will have been in the program for longer periods of time. If the program, as initially designed, was meant to be a temporary investment in the human capital of poor families, evaluation is required to determine whether the program is in fact improving those families' medium-term prospects, in the sense of allowing them to obtain better jobs, invest in projects with higher returns, or, more generally, generate a sustainable higher level of income through their own efforts. That may not be true for all families, and a household's demographic composition may be an important factor. But at least in a subset of cases, improvement should occur, and it is central to the poverty strategy to measure any improvements and to understand which conditions facilitate or hinder them. These are questions that could not be asked before but that become increasingly relevant as the program matures.

Two final remarks on evaluation are in order. First, in most cases results are presented as the percent change in a given variable as a result of the program—for example, the increase in high school enrollment. In many instances so far, those numbers have been "large" (in addition to statistically significant), meaning that on a percent basis there has been an important change in the variable. But the base on which the change is measured needs to be kept in mind, as in some cases a large variation may reflect a small base. That does not diminish the importance of the result. But two points are relevant. One is that a 50 percent increase in high school enrollment in a rural area, for example, might not necessarily be more significant than a 10 percent increase in the same variable in an urban area; it is simply that the base in rural areas is smaller since educational lags are larger, so that the rate of growth appears to be greater. Two is that over time it is natural to see a reduction in program impact when it is measured as a percentage of a given variable. But that need not imply that the program is less effective; it may indicate just that conditions become more difficult as the initial "easy" ground is covered.

To put it differently: a program focused on enhancing the human capital of the poor, by its very nature, needs a long time to fully achieve its objectives. And though "large" initial results might be encouraging, the fact that later results are not as notable need not mean that the program has become superfluous. It is therefore important to avoid generating expectations that will not be fulfilled over, say, the course of a *sexenio*—the nonrenewable six-year presidential term—and that actually may backfire; it is best to be more cautious and circumspect and to explain to all that a lengthy process is required to fully achieve the desired results.

The second remark concerns who does the evaluating. As discussed earlier, the program's administrative unit currently is in charge of both operational and impact evaluations. That arrangement needs to change. In order to establish a healthy division of labor and avoid potential conflicts of interest, program administrators should concentrate on administration and a separate unit should be charged with evaluation.

Need for Long-Term Institutional Stability

The preceding discussion can be summarized as assigning four tasks to those involved in managing Progresa-Oportunidades:

—to make necessary adjustments and corrections so that the program can continue to focus clearly on its objective of transferring income to the poor to enhance their human capital

—to avoid making the program more complex or adding more benefits that may distort beneficiaries' incentives

—to continue to conduct evaluations, including operational evaluations of the fulfillment of conditions

—to give the program sufficient time to fully achieve its objectives.

The program's current institutional set-up is unlikely to be able to support these tasks. Progresa-Oportunidades is a fragile program. With the leadership of two presidents and the commitment of a small set of officials from their administrations, much has been achieved over the course of ten years. But the special circumstances that have produced those achievements may change. At some point, a program like this needs to make the transition from relying on leaders and champions to establishing a more solid institutional set-up that is conducive to sustaining the effort over the long haul. Progresa-Oportunidades is at that point.

When the program was initially conceived, program designers argued against making the program's principles and benefits a matter of law.[3] Two main factors supported that decision: on one hand, given the novelty of the program and the uncertainty about its results, it was unduly risky to give the program formal legal status; on the other hand, it was irresponsible to legislate long-term benefits without having the budgetary resources to pay for them. As a result, the program's institutional framework was based on a combination of annual approval of resources and basic guidelines set forth in the budget decree, the more detailed operational rules based on the basic guidelines, and the creation by presidential decree of a new administrative unit to run the program.

That construct has served the program well, but it is not necessarily the best alternative for the future. On balance, one could argue that it has done what it could do and that given the objectives mentioned previously, a new construct is needed. The program has adapted in the past to changing circumstances; it needs to do so again.

The new construct need not be a law, although thought should be given to that possibility. But before suggesting a particular legal construct, it is essential to be clear about the aims. On one hand, experience has shown that legislating institutions and programs may have drawbacks: institutions have a way of remaining, while the objective of Progresa-Oportunidades is to eventually disappear. On the other hand, a carefully designed law could go a long way toward providing the stability and protection the program needs, and it also could contribute to strengthening operations if provisions on coordination and cooperation between ministries are incorporated. It also should address the issue of the separation of tasks between operations and evaluation. Similarly, a law could address the problem of program proliferation. Such a law would need to establish time periods for analysis and mechanisms to ensure that the program does not become a permanent program with permanent entitlements. It also would need to achieve the right balance between issuing detailed regulations to avoid the short-run political temptation to tinker

---

3. In Mexico, laws are different from both presidential decrees and decrees approved by only one of the chambers of Congress (like the budget decree). A law must be approved by both chambers and promulgated by the president; it creates entitlements that last for many years, until a new law modifies or eliminates them. The budget decree establishes only annual subsidies, not rights.

with the program and maintaining the flexibility to adjust the program's incentive structure as further evaluation results become available or as circumstances change.

In any event, any discussion concerning a legal proposal will in all likelihood not occur until the new administration takes over in December 2006. That discussion therefore would overlap with the program's third critical transition, which, as mentioned in the previous chapter, will occur in 2007: the next administration's decision regarding whether to continue the program. And, at least one more time, continuity will depend more on leadership and less on the existence of a solid institutional framework. Time will tell whether, in the context of Mexico's maturing democracy, the program's principles and objectives can be sustained.

The Need for Compatibility of Incentives in Social Policy

More than ten years ago, at the time Progresa-Oportunidades was being designed, Mexico undertook a major reform of its social security system. Since then various new social programs concerning health, job training, housing, education, and even pensions have been launched, some targeting poor workers from Progresa-Oportunidades families, some workers in the formal sector of the economy, and some workers in the informal sector. Other programs, in turn, grant benefits regardless of a recipient's form of participation in the labor market. It is probably fair to say that almost all of these programs and projects have been designed independently of the others.

But the distinctions drawn by bureaucracies among poor workers, informal sector workers, and formal sector workers, guided in many cases by a vertical view of ministries and agencies, do not necessarily reflect the reality of Mexican workers and Mexico's labor market. Some workers from Progresa-Oportunidades families are in the formal sector and therefore have access to social security benefits;[4] some who work in the formal sector do not receive social security benefits, as a result of large-scale evasion of social security legislation; and others do not and never will work in the formal sector because, for example, they are self-employed, working their own land. Furthermore, it is extremely difficult in practice to

4. The concept of social security in Mexico is much broader than in many other countries, particularly the United States. In includes the right to housing, health care, and daycare centers for children, among other benefits, as well as pensions.

correctly identify the potential beneficiaries of some of these programs, as workers move in and out of different jobs, some formal and some not.

Workers from Progresa-Oportunidades families who do have a formal sector job get benefits from both the program and the social security system, including pensions. Those who work in the informal sector or who are self-employed get the benefits of Progresa-Oportunidades, but they also have access to programs that provide health services, pensions, and housing that, while not formally equivalent to social security (in the sense of being entitlements), are nonetheless valuable in-kind transfers. These programs have their own eligibility rules and conditions. In some cases those conditions are implicit and in others, explicit. In fact, as things stand today, informal sector workers will lose some benefits that they obtain freely if they get a formal sector job with social security benefits.

The resulting incentive structure from this rather large set of programs is very complex, and its redistributive impact is not clear. But workers from Progresa-Oportunidades families do not care about that. From their perspective, there is a large set of social programs "out there," including Progresa-Oportunidades, and they make the best of them all. For those workers, the combination of free benefits from various social programs and the benefits of Progresa-Oportunidades might dominate the benefits of social security, given the wages that they could get in an informal or a formal sector job. Moreover, informal sector firms, or semi–formal sector firms evading social security, might be able to pay higher net wages than formal sector firms, as the latter have to include social security contributions in their labor costs while the former do not. Poor workers from program families might then end up in low-productivity informal sector jobs instead of high-productivity formal sector jobs, because the overall benefit packages of each alternative—wages and access to different social programs—are similar but labor costs to firms are not.

Locking poor workers in low-productivity jobs in the informal sector because the system creates perverse incentives is clearly not the best way to fight poverty. Poor families might be better off, but that result depends more on government cash and in-kind transfers than on their earned income. And if and when the transfers are removed, the welfare of those households will rapidly diminish. This is no longer a case in which "temporary investments in the human capital of the poor are made so that they can eventually pull out of poverty by their own efforts," which has been the objective of Progresa-Oportunidades since 1995. It is no longer the case not because of the program, but because the incentives offered by

Progresa-Oportunidades and those offered by other social programs for the poor are incompatible. Good intentions are trapping the poor in poverty. They also are making the economy less efficient.

Go back for a moment to figure 4-3 in chapter 4 and consider phase 6: program phase-down. The preceding discussion points out that, in a context of perverse incentives, phase-down might never occur. Not because of the program's design, but because of program proliferation and lack of policy coordination stemming from the vertical view of policy taken by ministries and agencies. Poor workers' improved health and higher education—the program's key to higher self-earned income in the future—may be counteracted by the incoherence of the incentive structure implicit in social policy. Poor workers' potentially increased productivity is not fully materialized, to the detriment of all.

These remarks hopefully throw more light on the issues of program proliferation and vertical policy design. They are not innocuous issues. They might be a way to solve a political problem for a president facing a divided Cabinet; they might be a way to demonstrate to the general public that the government is working "on many fronts" to help the poor; or they might be a way to ease approval of the federal budget as some additional members of Congress are brought on board by including a particular program for their community. But they are not the way to help the poor. The names of ministries and agencies—or the names of ministers, agency directors, or members of Congress—are not particularly relevant to the poor. All they see are programs that come and go—that today offer this benefit in exchange for that requirement but that tomorrow may not—and they just try to make the best of it. Who can blame them? They are just doing what anybody else would do under the same circumstances. One needs to ask here who exactly is expected to benefit from all these programs—government officials or poor workers?

In sum: program phase-down should not be seen as an event that occurs in a linear fashion over time after the program has been scaled up and operated for some period; it should be the result of a well-designed social policy that facilitates the entry of poor workers into the formal labor force and enables them, through their higher productivity, to earn higher incomes, making program benefits gradually unnecessary. Social policy must induce workers to seek higher-productivity jobs, not tax formal sector firms for creating them or subsidize informal firms that increase the number of low-productivity jobs. Social benefits for informal sector workers (including Progresa-Oportunidades workers) should not be so much better than those for formal sector workers (including Pro-gresa-Oportunidades workers) that taking a low-productivity job in the informal sector is better than taking a high-productivity job in the formal sector. But poor workers will search for high-productivity jobs—and for-mal sector firms will create them—only if incentives are well aligned and if Progresa-Oportunidades and other programs are designed as compo-nents of a single, coherent, and integrated social policy embedded in a horizontal view of policymaking. Program phase-down most probably will not occur as a self-contained phenomenon inside the program itself. Phase 6 in figure 4-3 is, from this perspective, a chimera.

The discussion ends here. Ten years ago when Progresa-Oportunidades was designed, it was considered by some to be a novel and innovative program that could make a decisive contribution to breaking the inter-generational transmission of poverty. But that assessment is incomplete. Despite its innovations, Progresa-Oportunidades was conceived as a poverty program embedded within an overall poverty strategy. That approach probably was better than before, but it is not enough. What was lacking then was sufficient understanding that, aside from the inter-nal coherence of the poverty strategy, overall coherence of the poverty strategy and broader social strategy also was required. Designing and operating a good poverty program within a poverty strategy is not the same as designing and operating a good program for the poor as part of a broader (and coherent) social policy strategy. This is not a minor semantic difference; it is a major substantive difference. If the latter is the case, program phase-down is automatic: it is part of program design, and it begins at the same time as program launch. Ensuring that Progresa and other social programs were consistent with each other was not done ten years ago; it needs to be done now. And if this book has a message, it is this: policymakers must not center their efforts only on the technical aspects of social policy, hard as that may be; from the beginning, the pro-grams that make up social policy should incorporate the key institutional features that are essential to making them successful.

CHAPTER SIX

Conclusions

Do poverty alleviation programs need a change of paradigm? That is too broad a question. The word "paradigm" is used here only to call attention to the fact that, at least in some cases, poverty alleviation programs that hope to have a notable and lasting impact on the poor need to incorporate into program design the elements needed to ensure scale-up, continuity, and sustainability. This book presents a case study of a particular program that has tried to do that: Mexico's Progresa-Oportunidades. Time will reveal the extent to which that goal was achieved, and it is others who should make the judgment.

Regardless of the program's merit, this book discusses how the program has attempted to incorporate those elements. It does so from two angles: first, from the perspective of the program's analytical components, including evaluation (chapters 1 to 3); second, from the perspective of program features that contributed to scale-up and continuity (chapters 4 and 5). Throughout, an effort has been made to combine the analytical arguments supporting the substantive content of Progresa-Oportunidades with the political economy considerations that influenced the decisions to start, scale up, and sustain the program. The book discusses how program designers and administrators incorporated both concerns at the beginning and during program development, shaping the program's institutional features accordingly. The central message of the book is that both must work together if the program is to be effective. An excellently designed but small and short-lived program is not truly useful, nor is a large, long-lived program that fails to achieve results.

This chapter concludes by making some observations that hopefully are supported by the preceding chapters. It is probably better not to call them policy recommendations. Conditions vary so much from country to country that a case-by-case analysis is required before concrete proposals can be made. Perhaps one could label them "observations cum suggestions," in the understanding that some of these observations and suggestions also apply to Progresa-Oportunidades. Ten follow.

One, a program that transfers income in cash and explicitly makes receipt of benefits contingent on some behavior that there appears to be reason to promote (otherwise known as a conditional cash transfer program) can make an important contribution to poverty alleviation. For reasons spelled out in chapters 1 and 2, such programs are much more efficient and effective than the diverse set of uncoordinated food subsidies, in-kind distributions of goods, price controls, and related instruments that have been used by many countries to increase poor households' income and food consumption. Further, under the right conditions, these programs might make themselves unnecessary in the future by helping beneficiaries make the transition from pure welfare today and pure welfare tomorrow to welfare with investment today and higher self-earned income tomorrow. But for that to occur, clarity is necessary regarding what problem needs to be solved; what the program is expected to do; what the program cannot and should not do; and how long it should take the program to do what it is supposed to do. It may seem obvious, but if there is no clear diagnosis or objectives, a new conditional cash transfer program may amount to nothing more than a government's response to a transient fashion in poverty programs worldwide.

Two, it is important from the beginning to have a vision regarding the scope and duration of the program. That does not mean an exact plan for each of its stages, but a general sense of the overall target population and reasonable estimates of the time that it should take to cover that population and the length of time that the program should be in place. Such projections help policymakers to estimate the administrative effort and the budgetary resources required as well as the institutional set-up needed. A vision also helps guide program development through the unpredictable but inevitable political and economic hurdles that appear along the way, serving as a compass in a long journey through uncharted territory.

Three, it is indispensable to incorporate into program design and operations those elements that can make a decisive contribution to program continuity. Assume that the program begins on day one of a new administration. At that point, the following question needs to be asked: under what conditions would the next administration, a certain number of years from today, be willing to continue with the program, assuming that the new administration and the current administration come from different political parties? The answer to this question will vary from country to country, but credibility, transparency, protection from political manipulation, and an effective public communications strategy are among the contributing factors that should be incorporated from the start.

It is important to note, however, that depending on a country's circumstances, incorporating those elements might involve more than minor technical adjustments to a program's modus operandi. New methods for selecting beneficiaries, arm's-length delivery of benefits, the absence of intermediaries, modest public communications campaigns, and so forth might represent a significant departure from the political traditions in a given country—traditions that have a reason, or at least had a reason, to exist. A trade-off between program sustainability and political feasibility (budgetary and operational considerations aside) might then be perceived. But that need not be the case; paradoxically, the political feasibility of sustaining the program might be crucially dependent on a new modus operandi. If so, the challenge would be to introduce the new modus operandi in a way that attracts the support of a sufficiently important coalition of political agents, even if other agents are net losers.

Four, the program must be sustainable from a budgetary point of view. Poverty programs, especially those concerned with a cumulative process like the formation of human capital, need long-term fiscal certainty. That is one reason, but not the only reason, to evaluate carefully whether the program is conceived as an addition to or as a replacement of existing programs. There may be a trade-off: while an addition may be politically easier in the initial stages of the program, a replacement increases the probability of program survival and facilitates program scale-up. Funding of social programs should not be a concern of the Finance Ministry alone; it needs to be a concern of program designers and administrators as well.

Five, the issues of program proliferation and compatibility of the incentives of different poverty programs with general social policy should be placed at the center of the agenda. Adding a new program to the existing set of programs (or adding new programs after the conditional cash transfer program is in place) may create a perverse incentive structure that hurts the poor. Even if there are no budgetary concerns, piling benefits on top of benefits does not help the poor. After some level of benefits is attained, in principle calibrated to ensure the effectiveness of the conditions of the program, any additional resources available for poverty alleviation will be much more effective if they are devoted to building infrastructure, enhancing the supply of services, or reinforcing productive programs. They should not be used to conduct more income transfers through parallel means that might end up locking the poor in low-productivity jobs. Although they are secondary, considerations about administrative capacity, possibilities for corruption, and the like point in the same direction. In devising poverty policy, it is perhaps useful to take note of a Mexican aphorism: *"poco y bueno"*—"few and good."

In incorporating the observations and suggestions offered above, a horizontal view of programs and projects should be promoted. Doing so effectively requires a policymaking process in which those in charge of social policy and those in charge of public finances are simultaneously present. The absence of such a process probably is an important reason for program proliferation. Simplifying and facilitating access to budget data on all programs and projects operated by the ministries and agencies involved in policy alleviation may contribute to controlling program proliferation. Making the evaluations of all such programs public (or making public the lack of evaluations) also may help. Simple incidence analysis or cost-benefit calculations showing that at times many programs barely provide benefits for the poor, although they do provide rents for others who are far from poor, may help as well. Making such analyses public may help even more.

Six, the incentives facing ministries, agencies, and officials need to be considered explicitly, particularly if the program requires coordination among ministries to achieve effective results (the need for coordination depends on the conditions for receipt of benefits). Ideally, all ministries and agencies would internalize the benefits of the program, and the resulting incentive alignment would produce an efficient outcome. But that does not happen often, and trade-offs need to be evaluated. Creating a new agency specifically to operate the new program might be a temporary solution to the problem, if it is given sufficient power, although its power might eventually erode as other ministries and agencies quietly or subtly block change. On the other hand, a drastic reorganization of tasks, budgets, and responsibilities across many ministries and agencies might divert attention and consume so much time and political capital that the program might not take off.

Whatever the solution, one must consider its sustainability, as agencies and ministries that are not among the winners vie for resources and space through the creation of new programs whose only real purpose, in the end, may be to prolong an agency's existence or increase a ministry's visibility. If, as is often the case, the solution to this problem is a temporary one, it must to be clear that it is temporary: if not, the lack of clarity will affect the objectives of the conditional cash transfer program (through program duplication and perversion of incentives), or its operations (as ministries and agencies center their attention on their own programs), or its sustainability (as budgetary resources are thinned out over many programs).

Seven, government officials' incentives for performing tasks require more attention. Effort and talent need to be distributed between program design (novel and interesting) and program operation (not so novel and not so interesting), in favor of the latter. But at times "recognition" (interpreted, in a broad sense, as promotion, exposure, travel, and the like) of task performance does not match the relative importance of the task. That may sound like a minor administrative concern; it is not. Given good program design, what really matters for the poor is that the program operate efficiently and that it do so for a long time. Program operation might eventually become boring, at least to some, but it will not become less important. Organizational changes are required to provide the right incentives to do the boring, or at least the no longer new, tasks (and changes in international financial institutions, which also like novel programs, also may be required).

Eight, evaluation is essential for program effectiveness; it can make an important contribution to program continuity; and it provides very useful information for making program adjustments. Ideally, evaluation is part of program design. Further, the program's data-gathering effort and scale-up strategy can be tailored to enhance the sturdiness of evaluations, permitting the use of experimental design methods, at least in the initial stages of the program. Combining quantitative and qualitative methods provides a rich source of information and a positive feedback loop among evaluation, program design, program operation, and program continuity. There is another essential role for evaluation: to ensure that the program is working. Little is gained by aligning agency and managerial incentives to continue operating a not-so-novel program that is not helping the poor. Evaluation is not an academic exercise, although involving the academic community might also contribute to program credibility.

Nine, use of international financial institutions (IFIs) should be considered to promote program continuity, not only program design, particularly during times of political change. As with much else, whether that is feasible depends highly on country circumstances. IFIs may, at the right time, express their support of a program to an incoming administration and perhaps commit resources if the new government continues with the program, particularly if the program has no significant negative characteristics (corruption, political misuse, and the like) and some notably positive ones (sensible design, efficient operation, good evaluations). If the IFI officials engaged in the program do not change during the transition period when national officials do, so much the better.

Program continuity and sustainability, on the other hand, might also impose some requirements on IFIs. As there is a growing awareness of the importance of these issues for poverty alleviation, all involved need to act accordingly. The remarks about interagency coordination, incentives for performing tasks, and the problem of vertical policymaking and program proliferation may also apply to these organizations. Clearly, it is not the task of IFIs to correct the domestic political problems that give rise to program proliferation and vertical policy design in the countries where they are engaged, but at the least, they should not make them worse. A careful loan portfolio within a given IFI and, even better, across IFIs would help; tactful and discreet advice would help as well; and consistency and persistence in giving policy advice that avoids fads and fashions would help even more.

Ten, continuity and sustainability require political leadership. It need not be there all the time, but it must be there at critical times. What is necessary are political leaders who understand that sustained poverty alleviation requires a long-term commitment from a society, not a regime; and statesmen who understand that what matters is the next generation, not the next election. In the end, what is needed are people who understand a simple fact: that poverty programs are more effective when the poor cease to be the subject of political discourse and become instead the subject of their own transformation. Everyone gains thereby.

References

Adato, Michelle, and others. 2000. *The Impact of PROGRESA on Women's Status and Intrahousehold Relations: A Final Report*. Washington: International Food Policy Research Institute.

Angelucci, Manuela. 2005. "Aid Programs' Unintended Effects: The Case of Progresa and Migration." University of Arizona, Department of Economics.

Angelucci, Manuela, Orazio Attanasio, and Jonathan Shaw. 2004. "El Efecto de Oportunidades sobre el Nivel y la Composición del Consumo en áreas Urbanas" ["The Effect of Oportunidades on the Level and Composition of Consumption in Urban Areas"]. In *Evaluación Externa de Impacto del Programa Oportunidades 2004: Aspectos Económicos y Sociales [External Evaluation of the Impact of the Program Oportunidades 2004: Economic and Social Aspects]*, edited by Bernardo Hernández Prado and Mauricio Hernández Ávila, vol. 4, chap. 2. Cuernavaca, Mexico: Instituto Nacional de Salud Pública.

Angelucci, Manuela, and Giacomo De Giorgi. 2006. "Indirect Effect of an Aid Program: The Case of Progresa and Consumption." Institute for the Study of Labor Discussion Paper 1955. Bonn, Germany.

Arias, Omar, and others. 2005. "Pending Issues in Protection, Productivity Growth, and Poverty Reduction." World Bank Policy Research Working Paper 3799, Latin America and Caribbean Region. Washington: World Bank.

Baltasar, Mary Carmen, and others. 2003. "Evaluación del Cumplimiento de Metas, Costos Unitarios, y Apego del Programa Oportunidades a las Reglas de Operación" ["Evaluation of the Fullfillment of Goals, Unit Costs, and Compliance with the Operational Rules of Oportunidades"]. In *Evaluación Externa de Impacto del Programa de Desarrollo Humano Oportunidades 2003 [External Evaluation of the Impact of the Human Development Program Oportunidades 2003]*, edited by Bernardo Hernández Prado and Mauricio Hernández Ávila, chap. 3. Cuernavaca, Mexico: Instituto Nacional de Salud Pública.

Barham, Tania. 2005. "Providing a Healthier Start to Life: The Impact of Conditional Cash Transfers on Infant Mortality." University of California at Berkeley, Department of Agriculture and Resource Economics.

Bautista, Sergio, and others. 2004. "Impacto de Oportunidades en la Morbilidad y el Estado de Salud de la Población Beneficiaria y en la Utilización de Servicios de Salud: Resultados de Corto Plazo en Zonas Urbanas y de Mediano Plazo en Zonas Rurales" ["Impact of Oportunidades on Morbidity and the Health Status of the Beneficiary Population and on the Use of Health Services: Short-Term Results in Urban Areas and Medium-Term Results in Rural Areas"]. In *Evaluación Externa de Impacto del Programa de Desarrollo Humano Oportunidades 2004: Salud* [*External Evaluation of the Impact of the Human Development Program Oportunidades 2004: Health*], edited by Bernardo Hernández Prado and Mauricio Hernández Ávila, vol. 2, chap. 1. Cuernavaca, Mexico: Instituto Nacional de Salud Pública.

Behrman, Jere, Benjamin Davis, and Emmanuel Skoufias. 1999. *Final Report: An Evaluation of the Selection of Beneficiary Households in the Education, Health, and Nutrition Program (PROGRESA) of Mexico.* Washington: International Food Policy Research Institute.

Behrman, Jere, and John Hoddinott. 2000. *An Evaluation of the Impact of PRO-GRESA on Pre-School Child Height.* Washington: International Food Policy Research Institute.

Behrman, Jere, Susan Parker, and Petra Todd. 2004. "Impacto de Mediano Plazo del Paquete de Oportunidades, Incluyendo el Aspecto Nutricional, sobre la Educación de Niños Rurales que Tenían entre 0 y 8 Años de Edad en 1997" ["Evaluation of the Medium-Term Impact of Oportunidades, Including Its Nutritional Aspects, on the Education of Rural Children Who Were 0 to 8 Years Old in 1997"]. In *Evaluación Externa de Impacto del Programa Oportunidades 2004: Educación* [*External Evaluation of the Impact of the Program Oportunidades 2004: Education*], edited by Bernardo Hernández Prado and Mauricio Hernández Ávila, vol. 1, chap. 2. Cuernavaca, Mexico: Instituto Nacional de Salud Pública.

Behrman, Jere, Piyali Sengupta, and Petra Todd. 2000. *The Impact of PRO-GRESA on Achievement Test Scores in the First Year: Final Report.* Washington: International Food Policy Research Institute.

———. 2001. *Progressing through PROGRESA: An Impact Assessment of a School Subsidy Experiment.* University of Pennsylvania and the International Food Policy Research Institute.

Behrman, Jere, and Petra Todd. 1999a. *A Report on the Sample Sizes used for the Evaluation of the Education, Health, and Nutrition Program (PROGRESA) of Mexico.* Washington: International Food Policy Research Institute.

———. 1999b. *Randomness in the Experimental Samples of PROGRESA (Education, Health and Nutrition Program).* Washington: International Food Policy Research Institute.

Besley, Timothy, and Ravi Kanbur. 1988. "Food Subsidies and Poverty Alleviation." *Economic Journal* 98, no. 392: 701–19.

————. 1990. "The Principles of Targeting." Policy Research Working Paper Series 385. Washington: World Bank.

Cabral, J., and others. 2002. "Evaluación del Impacto del Programa de Educación, Salud, y Alimentación (Progresa) en el Estado de Nutrición de los Niños Menores de 5 Años que Viven en Localidades Atendidas por IMSS-Solidaridad" ["Evaluation of the Impact of the Education, Health, and Food Program (Progresa) on the Nutritional Status of Children Younger than Five Years Old in Localities Served by IMSS-Solidaridad"]. In *Las Múltiples Facetas de la Investigación en Salud 2: Proyectos Estratégicos del Instituto Mexicano del Seguro Social* [*The Multiple Facets of Health Research 2: Strategic Projects of the Mexican Institute of Social Security*], pp. 175–94. Mexico City: Instituto Mexicano del Seguro Social.

Carter, Michael, and Christopher Barret. 2006. "The Economics of Poverty Traps and Persistent Poverty: An Asset-Based Approach." *Journal of Development Studies* 42, no. 2: 178–99.

Coady, David, and Susan Parker. 2004. "Evaluación del Mecanismo de Focalización de Oportunidades en Zonas Urbanas" ["Evaluation of the Oportunidades Targeting Mechanism in Urban Areas"]. In *Evaluación Externa de Impacto del Programa Oportunidades 2004: Aspectos Económicos y Sociales* [*External Evaluation of the Impact of the Program Oportunidades 2004: Economic and Social Aspects*], edited by Bernardo Hernández Prado and Mauricio Hernández Ávila, vol. 4, chap. 5. Cuernavaca, Mexico: Instituto Nacional de Salud Pública.

Cortes, Fernando, Patricio Solís, and Israel Banegas. 2006. "Oportunidades y Pobreza en México: 2002–2004" ["Oportunidades and Poverty in Mexico: 2002–2004"]. Mexico City: El Colegio de México.

Dávila, Enrique, and Santiago Levy. 1996. "Tiendas Diconsa y Política Social" ["Diconsa Stores and Social Policy"]. Working Paper. Mexico City: Secretaría de Hacienda y Crédito Público.

————. 2003. "Taxing for Equity: A Proposal to Reform Mexico's Value-Added Tax." In *Latin American Macroeconomic Reforms: The Second Stage*, edited by Jose Antonio González and others, pp. 357–92. University of Chicago Press.

————. 2004. "Pobreza y Dispersion Poblacional en Mexico ["Poverty and Population Dispersion in Mexico]." In *Ensayos sobre el Desarrollo Economico y Social de Mexico* [*Essays on the Economic and Social Development of Mexico*], edited by Santiago Levy, pp. 152–180. Mexico City: Fondo de Cultura Economica.

Davis, Benjamin, Ashu Handa, and Humberto Soto. 2001. "Crisis, Poverty, and Long-Term Development: Examining the Mexican Case." FAO, IDB, and PROGRESA (August).

De Alba, Enrique, Javier Alagón, and Antonio Villa. 1997. "Evaluación del Proyecto Piloto de Nutrición, Alimentación, y Salud" ["Evaluation of the Pilot Project on Nutrition, Food, and Health"]. In *Pobreza y Política Social en México* [*Poverty and Social Policy in Mexico*], edited by Gabriel Martinez, in

Lecturas del Trimestre Económico 85. Mexico City: Instituto Tecnológico Autónomo de México y Fondo de Cultura Económica.

Dresser, Denise. 1994. "Pronasol y Política: Combate a la Pobreza como Formula de Gobernabilidad" ["Pronasol and Politics: Poverty Alleviation as a Formula for Governability"]. In *La Pobreza en México: Causas y Políticas para Combatirla* [*Poverty in Mexico: Causes and Policies to Combat It*], in Lecturas del Trimestre Economico 78, compiled by Felix Vélez, pp. 262–99. Mexico City: Instituto Tecnológico Autónomo de México y Fondo de Cultura Económica.

Duarte, Maria Beatriz, and others. 2004. "Impacto de Oportunidades sobre los Conocimientos y Practicas de Madres Beneficiarias y Jóvenes Becarios: Una Evaluación de las Sesiones Educativas para la Salud" ["Impact of Oportunidades on the Knowledge and Practices of Beneficiary Mothers and Youngsters with Scholarships: An Evaluation of the Educational Health Talks"]. In *Evaluación Externa de Impacto del Programa Oportunidades 2004: Salud* [*External Evaluation of the Impact of the Program Oportunidades 2004: Health*], edited by Bernardo Hernández Prado and Mauricio Hernández Ávila, pp. 247–330, vol. 2, chap. 6. Cuernavaca, Mexico: Instituto Nacional de Salud Pública.

Escobar Latapi, Agustin, and Mercedez González de la Rocha. 2000. "Logros y Retos: Una Evaluación Cualitativa de Progresa en México" ["Achievements and Challenges: A Qualitative Evaluation of Progresa in Mexico"]. In *Evaluación de Resultados del Programa de Educación, Salud, y Alimentación: Impacto a Nivel Comunitario* [*Evaluation of Results of the Program of Education, Health, and Food: Impact at the Community Level*], pp. 1–132. Washington: International Food Policy Research Institute.

———. 2003. "Evaluación Cualitativa del Programa Oportunidades en Zonas Urbanas 2003" ["Qualitative Evaluation of the Program Oportunidades in Urban Areas 2003"]. In *Evaluación Externa de Impacto del Programa Oportunidades 2003* [*External Evaluation of the Impact of the Program Oportunidades 2003*], edited by Bernardo Hernández Prado and Mauricio Hernández Ávila, chap. 4. Cuernavaca, Mexico: Instituto Nacional de Salud Pública.

———. 2004. "Evaluación Cualitativa de Mediano Plazo del Programa Oportunidades en Zonas Rurales" ["Qualitative Medium-Term Evaluation of Oportunidades in Rural Areas"]. In *Evaluación Externa de Impacto del Programa Oportunidades 2004: Aspectos Económicos y Sociales* [*External Evaluation of the Impact of the Program Oportunidades 2004: Economic and Social Aspects*], edited by Bernardo Hernández Prado and Mauricio Hernández Ávila, vol. 4, chap. 6. Cuernavaca, Mexico: Instituto Nacional de Salud Pública.

Fernald, Lia, Paul Gertler, and Gustavo Olaiz. 2004. "Impacto de Mediano Plazo del Programa Oportunidades sobre la Obesidad y las Enfermedades Crónicas en Áreas Rurales" ["Medium-Term Impact of Oportunidades on Obesity and Chronic Diseases in Rural Areas"]. In *Evaluación Externa de Impacto del Programa Oportunidades 2004: Salud* [*External Evaluation of the Impact of the Program Oportunidades 2004: Health*], edited by Bernardo Hernández Prado and Mauricio Hernández Ávila, pp. 247–330, vol. 2, chap. 6. Cuernavaca, Mexico: Instituto Nacional de Salud Pública.

Gertler, Paul. 2000. *Final Report: The Impact of PROGRESA on Health.* Washington: International Food Policy Research Institute.

Gertler, Paul, and Lia Fernald. 2004. "Impacto de Mediano Plazo del Programa Oportunidades sobre el Desarrollo Infantil en Áreas Rurales" ["Medium-Term Impact of Oportunidades on Child Development in Rural Areas"]. In *Evaluación Externa de Impacto del Programa Oportunidades 2004: Alimentación* [*External Evaluation of the Impact of the Program Oportunidades 2004: Food*], edited by Bernardo Hernández Prado and Mauricio Hernández Ávila, vol. 3, chap. 2. Cuernavaca, Mexico: Instituto Nacional de Salud Pública.

Gertler, Paul, Sebastián Martinez, and Marta Rubio. 2005. "El Efecto de Oportunidades sobre el Incremento en el Consumo de los Hogares a partir de Inversiones Productivas en Microempresas y Produccion Agrícola" ["The Effect of Oportunidades on the Increase in Household Consumption as a Result of Productive Investments in Microenterprises and Agricultural Production"]. In *Evaluacion Externa de Impacto del Programa Oportunidades 2004. Aspectos Económicos y Sociales* [*External Evaluation of the Impact of the Program Oportunidades 2004: Economic and Social Aspects*], edited by Bernardo Hernández Prado and Mauricio Hernández Ávila, pp. 105–54. Cuernavaca, Mexico: Instituto Nacional de Salud Pública.

Gómez de León, Jose. 1998. "Dimensiones Correlativas de la Pobreza en México: Elementos para la Focalización de Programas Sociales" ["Correlated Dimensions of Poverty in Mexico: Elements for Targeting by Social Programs"]. Paper presented at la Red LACEA/BID/Banco Mundial sobre Desigualdad y Pobreza, Buenos Aires, October 21–24, 1998.

Gutiérrez, Juan Pablo, and others. 2004a. "Impacto de Oportunidades en los Comportamientos de Riesgo de los Adolescentes y en sus Consecuencias Inmediatas: Resultados de Corto Plazo en Zonas Urbanas y de Mediano Plazo en Zonas Rurales" ["Impact of Oportunidades on Adolescent Risk Behavior and on Its Immediate Consequences: Short-Term Results in Urban Areas and Medium-Term Results in Rural Areas"]. In *Evaluación Externa de Impacto del Programa Oportunidades 2004: Salud* [*External Evaluation of the Impact of the Program Oportunidades 2004: Health*], edited by Bernardo Hernández Prado and Mauricio Hernández Ávila, vol. 2, chap. 2. Cuernavaca, Mexico: Instituto Nacional de Salud Pública.

———. 2004b. "Impacto de Oportunidades en la Morbilidad y el Estado de la Salud de la Población Beneficiaria y en la Utilización de Servicios de Salud: Resultados de Corto Plazo en las Zonas Urbanas y de Mediano Plazo en Zonas Rurales" ["Impact of Oportunidades on Morbidity, Health Status, and Use of Health Services by the Beneficiary Population: Short-Term Results in Urban Areas and Medium-Term Results in Rural Areas"]. In *Evaluación Externa de Impacto del Programa Oportunidades 2004: Salud* [*External Evaluation of the Impact of the Program Oportunidades 2004: Health*], edited by Bernardo Hernández Prado and Mauricio Hernández Ávila, vol. 2, chap. 1. Cuernavaca, Mexico: Instituto Nacional de Salud Pública.

Hernández, Bernardo, and others. 2003. "Evaluación del Impacto de Oportunidades en la Mortalidad Materna e Infantil" ["Evaluation of the Impact of

Oportunidades on Infant and Maternal Mortality"]. In *Evaluación Externa de Impacto del Programa Oportunidades 2003* [*External Evaluation of the Impact of the Program Oportunidades 2003*], edited by Bernardo Hernández Prado and Mauricio Hernández Ávila, vol. 2, chap. 2. Cuernavaca, Mexico: Instituto Nacional de Salud Pública.

————. 2004. "Impacto de Oportunidades en la Salud Reproductiva de la Población Beneficiaria" ["Impact of Oportunidades on Reproductive Health of the Beneficiary Population"]. In *Evaluación Externa de Impacto del Programa Oportunidades 2004: Salud* [*External Evaluation of the Impact of the Program Oportunidades 2004: Health*], edited by Bernardo Hernández Prado and Mauricio Hernández Ávila, vol. 2, chap. 3. Cuernavaca, Mexico: Instituto Nacional de Salud Pública.

Hernández, Daniel, and Maria del Carmen Huerta. 2000. "Algunos Aspectos de Salud Reproductiva de la Población Beneficiaria de Progresa" ["Some Aspects of Reproductive Health in Progresa's Beneficiary Population"]. In *Evaluación de Resultados del Programa de Educación, Salud, y Alimentación* [*Evaluation of Results of the Program of Education, Health, and Food*], pp. 43–80. Washington: International Food Policy Research Institute.

Hernández, Daniel, Monica Orozco, and Daniela Sotres. 2000. "El Impacto de Progresa en la Inscripción a la Secundaria: Datos de Multinivel de la Matricula Escolar" ["Impact of Progresa on Secondary-School Registration: Multilevel Data from School Registration Rolls"]. In *Evaluación de Resultados del Programa de Educación, Salud, y Alimentación* [*Evaluation of Results of the Program of Education, Health, and Food*], pp. 185–205. Washington: International Food Policy Research Institute.

Hoddinott, John, Emmanuel Skoufias, and Ryan Washburn. 2000. *The Impact of PROGRESA on Consumption: A Final Report.* Washington: International Food Policy Research Institute.

Huerta, Maria del Carmen, and Homero Martínez. 2000. "Evaluación del Impacto de Progresa en el Estado de Nutrición de los Menores de 5 años en Localidades Atendidas por IMSS-Solidaridad" ["Evaluation of the Impact of Progresa on the Nutritional Status of Children under Five in Localities Served by IMSS-Solidaridad"]. In *Evaluación de Resultados del Programa de Educación, Salud, y Alimentación* [*Evaluation of Results of the Program of Education, Health, and Food*], p. 149–206. Washington: International Food Policy Research Institute.

Instituto Nacional de Salud Pública. 2001. "Evaluación de Impacto del Programa de Educación, Salud, y Alimentación en el Estado Nutricio del Niño: Primera Evaluación Anual" ["Evaluation of the Food, Health, and Education Program on the Nutritional Status of Children: First Annual Evaluation"]. Working Paper. Cuernavaca, Mexico.

Levy, Santiago. 1994. "La Pobreza en México" ["Poverty in Mexico"]. In *La Pobreza en México: Causas y Políticas para Combatirla* [*Poverty in Mexico: Causes and Policies to Combat It*], in Lecturas del Trimestre Economico 78, compiled by Felix Vélez, pp. 15–112. Mexico City: Instituto Tecnológico Autónomo de México y Fondo de Cultura Económica.

————. 1997. "Presupuesto y Politica Social." *Nexos* 20, no. 239: 7–10.

————. 2000. "El Presupuesto de Egresos de la Federación: Transparencia, Discrecionalidad, y Eficiencia" ["The Federal Expenditure Budget: Transparency, Discretionary Authority, and Efficiency"]. *Este País* 115 (October): 2–14.

Levy, Santiago, and Evelyne Rodriguez. 2004. "Economic Crisis, Political Transition, and Poverty Policy Reform: Mexico's Progresa-Oportunidades Program." Policy Dialogue Series. Washington: Inter-American Development Bank.

Levy, Santiago, and Sweder van Wijnbergen. 1992. "Maize and the Mexico–United States Free Trade Agreement." *World Bank Economic Review* 6, no. 3: 481–503.

————. 1994. "Labor Markets, Migration, and Welfare Agriculture in the North American Free Trade Agreement." *Journal of Development Economics* 43, no. 2: 263–78.

————. 1995. "Transition Problems in Economic Reform: Agriculture in the North American Free Trade Agreement." *American Economic Review* 85, no. 4: 738–54.

Lipton, Michael, and Martin Ravallion. 1995. "Poverty and Policy." In *Handbook of Development Economics*, vol. 3, part 2, edited by Jere Behrman and T. N. Srinivasan, pp. 2551–657. Amsterdam: North-Holland Press.

Lustig, Nora Claudia. 1984. "Distribution of Income, Food Consumption, and Alternative Policy Options." In *The Political Economy of Income Distribution in Mexico*, edited by Pedro Aspe and Paul Sigmund. New York: Holmes and Meier Publishers.

Meneses, Fernando, and others. 2003. "Evaluación del Cumplimiento de Metas, Costos Unitarios, y Apego del Programa Oportunidades a las Reglas de Operación" ["Evaluation of the Fullfillment of Goals, Unit Costs, and Compliance with the Operational Rules of Oportunidades"]. In *Evaluación Externa de Impacto del Programa Oportunidades 2003 [External Evaluation of the Impact of the Program Oportunidades 2003]*, edited by Bernardo Hernández Prado and Mauricio Hernández Ávila, chap. 3. Cuernavaca, Mexico: Instituto Nacional de Salud Pública.

Meneses, Fernando, and others. 2004. "Evaluación del Cumplimiento de Metas, Costos Unitarios, y Apego del Programa a las Reglas de Operación 2004 ["Evaluation of the Fullfillment of Goals, Unit Costs, and Compliance with the Operational Rules of Oportunidades"]. In *Evaluación Externa de Impacto del Programa Oportunidades 2004 [External Evaluation of the Impact of the Program Oportunidades 2004]*, edited by Bernardo Hernández Prado and Mauricio Hernández Ávila, vol. 4, chap. 7. Cuernavaca, Mexico: Instituto Nacional de Salud Pública.

Narayan, Deepa, and others. 2000. *Voices of the Poor: Can Anyone Hear Us?* New York: Oxford University Press.

Neufeld, Lynnette, and others. 2004a. "Impacto de Oportunidades en el Crecimiento y Estado Nutricional de Niños en Zonas Rurales" ["Impact of Oportunidades on Growth and Nutritional Status of Children in Rural Areas"]. In *Evaluación Externa de Impacto del Programa Oportunidades 2004: Alimentación [External Evaluation of the Impact of the Program Oportunidades*

2004: Food], edited by Bernardo Hernández Prado and Mauricio Hernández Ávila, vol. 3, chap. 1. Cuernavaca, Mexico: Instituto Nacional de Salud Pública.

————. 2004b. "Estudio Comparativo sobre el Estado Nutricional y la Adquisición de Lenguaje entre Niños de Localidades Urbanas con y sin Oportunidades" ["Comparative Study of Nutritional Status and Language Acquisition among Children in Urban Localitites with and without Oportunidades"]. In *Evaluación Externa de Impacto del Programa Oportunidades 2004: Alimentación* [*External Evaluation of the Impact of the Program Oportunidades 2004: Food*], edited by Bernardo Hernández Prado and Mauricio Hernández Ávila, vol. 3, chap. 3. Cuernavaca, Mexico: Instituto Nacional de Salud Pública.

————. 2004c. "Estudio sobre el Consumo de los Suplementos Alimenticios Nutrisano y Nutrivida en Niños y Mujeres de Zonas Urbanas Beneficiarios de Oportunidades" ["Study of the Consumption of the Nutritional Supplements Nutrisano and Nutrivida by Children and Women Beneficiaries of Oportunidades in Urban Areas"]. In *Evaluación Externa de Impacto del Programa Oportunidades 2004: Alimentación* [*External Evaluation of the Impact of the Program Oportunidades 2004: Food*], edited by Bernardo Hernández Prado and Mauricio Hernández Ávila, vol. 3, chap. 4. Cuernavaca, Mexico: Instituto Nacional de Salud Pública.

Oportunidades. 2005a. *Evaluación Externa de Impacto del Programa Oportunidades 2003* [*External Evaluation of the Impact of the Program Oportunidades 2003*], edited by Bernardo Hernández Prado and Mauricio Hernández Ávila. Cuernavaca, Mexico: Instituto Nacional de Salud Pública.

————. 2005b. *Evaluación Externa de Impacto del Programa Oportunidades 2004: Educación* [*External Evaluation of the Impact of the Program Oportunidades 2004: Education*], edited by Bernardo Hernández Prado and Mauricio Hernández Ávila. Cuernavaca, Mexico: Instituto Nacional de Salud Pública.

————. 2005c. *Evaluación Externa de Impacto del Programa Oportunidades 2004: Salud* [*External Evaluation of the Impact of the Program Oportunidades 2004: Health*], edited by Bernardo Hernández Prado and Mauricio Hernández Ávila, vol. 2. Cuernavaca, Mexico: Instituto Nacional de Salud Pública.

————. 2005d. *Evaluación Externa de Impacto del Programa Oportunidades 2004: Alimentación* [*External Evaluation of the Impact of the Program Oportunidades 2004: Food*], edited by Bernardo Hernández Prado and Mauricio Hernández Ávila, vol. 3. Cuernavaca, Mexico: Instituto Nacional de Salud Pública.

————. 2005e. *Evaluación Externa de Impacto del Programa Oportunidades 2004: Aspectos Económicos y Sociales* [*External Evaluation of the Impact of the Program Oportunidades 2004: Economic and Social Aspects*], edited by Bernardo Hernández Prado and Mauricio Hernández Ávila, vol. 4. Cuernavaca, Mexico: Instituto Nacional de Salud Pública.

Parker, Susan. 2003. "Evaluación del Impacto de Oportunidades sobre la Inscripción Escolar: Primaria, Secundaria, y Media Superior" ["Impact of Oportunidades on School Enrollment: Primary, Secondary and High School"]. In

Resultados de la Evaluación Externa del Programa de Desarrollo Humano Oportunidades: 2002 [*Results of the External Evaluation of the Human Development Program Oportunidades: 2002*]. Mexico City: Secretaría de Desarrollo Social.

———. 2005. "Evaluación del Impacto de Oportunidades sobre la Inscripción, Reprobación, y Abandono Escolar" ["Evaluation of the Impact of Oportunidades on Enrollment, Failure, and Drop-Out Rates"]. In *Evaluación Externa de Impacto del Programa Oportunidades 2003* [*External Evaluation of the Impact of the Program Oportunidades 2003*], edited by Bernardo Hernández Prado and Mauricio Hernández Ávila, chap. 1. Cuernavaca, Mexico: Instituto Nacional de Salud Pública.

Parker, Susan, Jere Behrman, and Petra Todd. 2005. "Impacto de Mediano Plazo del Programa Oportunidades sobre la Educación y el Trabajo de Jóvenes del Medio Rural que Tenían de 9 a 15 Años de Edad en 1997" ["Medium-Term Impact of Oportunidades on Education and Work of Youngsters in Rural Areas between Nine and Fifteen Years Old in 1997"]. In *Evaluación Externa de Impacto del Programa Oportunidades 2004: Educación* [*External Evaluation of the Impact of the Program Oportunidades 2004: Education*], edited by Bernardo Hernández Prado and Mauricio Hernández Ávila, vol. 1, chap. 1. Cuernavaca, Mexico: Instituto Nacional de Salud Pública.

Parker, Susan, and Emmanuel Skoufias. 2000. *The Impact of PROGRESA on Work, Leisure, and Time Allocation: Final Report.* Washington: International Food Policy Research Institute.

———. 2001. "Conditional Cash Transfers and Their Impact on Child Work and Schooling: Evidence from the PROGRESA Program in Mexico." FCND Discussion Paper 123. Washington: International Food Policy Research Institute.

Rubalcava, Luis, and Graciela Teruel. 2005. "El Efecto de Oportunidades sobre la Dinámica Demográfica de los Hogares Beneficiaries y las Desiciones de Migración de sus Integrantes, en Localidades Rurales" ["The Effects of Oportunidades on the Demographic Dynamics of Beneficiary Households in Rural Areas and the Migration Decisions of Their Members"]. In *Evaluación Externa de Impacto del Programa Oportunidades 2004: Aspectos Económicos y Sociales* [*External Evaluation of the Impact of the Program Oportunidades 2004: Economic and Social Aspects*], edited by Bernardo Hernández Prado and Mauricio Hernández Ávila, vol. 4, chap. 4. Cuernavaca, Mexico: Instituto Nacional de Salud Pública.

Schultz, Paul. 2000a. *The Impact of PROGRESA on School Enrollments. Final Report.* Washington: International Food Policy Research Institute.

———. 2000b. *Impact of PROGRESA on School Attendance Rates in the Sampled Population.* Washington: International Food Policy Research Institute.

Secretaría de la Contraloría y Desarrollo Administrativo. 1996. "*Evaluación de la Prueba Piloto del Programa: Canasta Básica Alimentaria para el Bienestar de la Familia en el Estado de Campeche*" ["Evaluation of the Pilot Program: Basic Food Basket for Family Welfare in the State of Campeche"]. Working Paper (August).

Secretaría de Desarrollo Social. 2005. *Medición de la Pobreza 2002–2004 [Measurement of Poverty, 2002–2004]*. Mexico City: Comité Técnico para la Medición de la Pobreza en México.

Secretaría de Hacienda y Crédito Público. 1998. *Exposición de Motivos del Proyecto de Presupuesto de Egresos de la Federación 1999 [The President's Federal Expenditure Budget Proposal for 1999]*. Mexico City.

————. 1999. *Exposición de Motivos del Proyecto de Presupuesto de Egresos de la Federación 2000 [The President's Federal Expenditure Budget Proposal for 2000]*. Mexico City.

————. 2000. *Exposición de Motivos del Proyecto de Presupuesto de Egresos de la Federación 2001 [The President's Federal Expenditure Budget Proposal for 2001]*. Mexico City.

Skoufias, Emmanuel. 2000. *Is PROGRESA Working? Summary of the Results of an Evaluation by IFPRI*. Washington: International Food Policy Research Institute.

————. 2005. "PROGRESA and Its Impacts on the Welfare of Rural Households in Mexico." Research Report 139. Washington: International Food Policy Research Institute.

Streeten, Paul. 1989. "Hunger." Discussion Paper 4. Boston University, Institute for Economic Development.

Todd, Petra, and others. 2005. "Impacto de Oportunidades sobre la Educación de Niños y Jóvenes de Áreas Urbanas después de un Año de Participación en el Programa" ["Impact of Oportunidades on the Education of Children and Youngsters in Urban Areas after One Year of Participation in the Program"]. In *Evaluación Externa de Impacto del Programa Oportunidades 2004: Educación [External Evaluation of the Impact of the Program Oportunidades 2004: Education]*, edited by Bernardo Hernández Prado and Mauricio Hernández Ávila, vol. 1, chap. 3. Cuernavaca, Mexico: Instituto Nacional de Salud Pública.

World Bank. 2003. *World Development Report 2004: Making Services Work for Poor People*. Oxford University Press.

————. 2004. *Pobreza en México: Una Evaluación de las Condiciones, las Tendencias, y la Estrategia del Gobierno [Poverty in Mexico: An Evaluation of Conditions, Tendencies, and the Government's Strategy]*. Banco Mundial–México.

————. 2005. *World Development Report 2006: Equity and Development*. Oxford University Press.

Index

Centro de Investigacion y Estudios Superiores en Antropología Social (CIESAS) (Center for Research and Advanced Studies in Social Anthropology), 43, 70
Cervical cancer screening, 57–58
Children: health and nutritional status, impact on, 52–55; infant mortality, 8–9, 11, 51–52; labor market participation, 64; prenatal care, impact of, 51. *See also* Education; Infant mortality
CIESAS. *See* Centro de Investigacion y Estudios Superiores en Antropología Social
Community participation, absence of, 99
Complementarities and behavioral contingencies, 123–25
Conceptual consistency, 134–35
Conditional benefits and program replication, 123–25
Conflicts of interest, avoiding, 139
Congress: and budget information, 109; and democratic transition, 104; and food subsidy elimination, 105; and political neutrality of program, 102, 107–8
Consistency, need for, 134–36
Consumption impact, 44–46, 47
Continuity. *See* Sustainability and continuity
Contraception and family planning, 9, 57, 58
Core program elements, 127–30
Credibility, 43–44, 101–7, 126–27

Data gathering and analysis: capabilities for, 91–92; and continuous evaluation, 136; for quantitative evaluation, 37–42
Democratic environment, 99, 101–6
Demographic composition of households, 72–73
Demographic dynamics and sustainability, 131–34

Dependence on assistance: avoidance of, 10, 13, 24; gradualism and risk of, 82
Development phases, 115–18
Diabetes, 57
Diconsa, 79
Difference in difference, 39–40
Discretion, 102–3
Disease, 52, 56–57
Distribution of beneficiaries by age and gender, 131–34
Distribution of households, geographical, 27, 85–86
Double difference estimation, 39–40
Drinking by adolescents, 55
Dropout rates, 63–64

Econometric techniques, 37–38, 79. *See also* Evaluation design and methods
Economic crisis (*1994–95*), 13–15
Economic growth and demographic dynamics, 133–34
Economic shocks, insulation from, 68–69, 125–26
Education: absenteeism, 65; benefits, 23; and demographic dynamics, 132–34; differential program incorporation and impacts on, 60–62; dropout, failure, and repeat rates, 63–64; enrollment impacts, 58–60; family size and health, interactions with, 11; in mid-*1990s*, 9–10; and migration, 75; post–high school transition, 137–38; quality measurement, 137; standardized testing and attainment impacts, 62–63
Electoral pressures, protection from, 107–08
Empowerment of beneficiaries, 17, 111–12
Engel's Law, 45
Escobar Lapti, Agustin, 71–72
Evaluation design and methods: basis of measurement, 138–39;